CW00674907

Grandparenting the Children of Addicted Parents

of related interest

Inside Kinship Care
Understanding Family Dynamics
and Providing Effective Support
Edited by David Pitcher
Foreword by Bob Broad
ISBN 978 1 84905 346 4
eISBN 978 0 85700 682 0

The A–Z of Therapeutic Parenting
Strategies and Solutions
Sarah Naish
ISBN 978 1 78592 376 0
eISBN 978 1 78450 732 9

Healing the Hidden Hurts
Transforming Attachment and
Trauma Theory into Effective Practice
with Families, Children and Adults
*Edited by Caroline Archer,
Charlotte Drury and Jude Hills*
ISBN 978 1 84905 548 2
eISBN 978 0 85700 972 2

The Simple Guide to Child Trauma
What It Is and How to Help
Betsy de Thierry
Illustrated by Emma Reeves
Foreword by David Shemmings
ISBN 978 1 78592 136 0
eISBN 978 1 78450 401 4

Grandparenting the Children of Addicted Parents
Experiences and Wisdom for Kinship Carers

Edited by Janet Bujra
with The Grandparents Group

Foreword by Nigel Priestley
Afterword by Caroline Archer

Jessica Kingsley *Publishers*
London and Philadelphia

First published in 2019
by Jessica Kingsley Publishers
73 Collier Street
London N1 9BE, UK
and
400 Market Street, Suite 400
Philadelphia, PA 19106, USA

www.jkp.com

Copyright © Jessica Kingsley Publishers 2019
Foreword copyright © Nigel Priestley 2019
Afterword copyright © Caroline Archer 2019

All rights reserved. No part of this publication may be reproduced in any
material form (including photocopying, storing in any medium by electronic
means or transmitting) without the written permission of the copyright owner
except in accordance with the provisions of the law or under terms of a licence
issued in the UK by the Copyright Licensing Agency Ltd. www.cla.co.uk or in
overseas territories by the relevant reproduction rights organisation, for details
see www.ifrro.org. Applications for the copyright owner's written permission
to reproduce any part of this publication should be addressed to the publisher.

Warning: The doing of an unauthorised act in relation to a copyright work
may result in both a civil claim for damages and criminal prosecution.

Library of Congress Cataloging in Publication Data
A CIP catalog record for this book is available from the Library of Congress

British Library Cataloguing in Publication Data
A CIP catalogue record for this book is available from the British Library

ISBN 978 1 78592 539 9
eISBN 978 1 78450 947 7

Printed and bound in Great Britain

For all the caring and dedicated grandparents
who are raising traumatised children.

Contents

Foreword

Nigel Priestley

Nigel Priestley is a senior partner at Ridley and Hall Legal Ltd solicitors in Huddersfield. He has acted in many cases where grandparents are claiming rights to financial support or protection for the grandchildren they are raising. A campaigner for many years in this field, he has addressed groups and offered information and support. He is also an adoptive parent who knows at first hand the traumatic effect on children of parental loss. He writes a regular column for Adoption UK's magazine, *Adoption Today*.

* * *

It is the Friday night phone call that many grandparents fear. It mostly goes something like this: 'It's Charlene's social worker here. If you don't come and collect Jemima now, she'll have to go into foster care. She can't stay here.'

At that moment, lives are changed. Many grandparents find themselves in a legal jungle with no obvious paths and no maps. What are they to do about work, child care, the behaviour of the child, contact with the birth parents and financial support? Who can they ask? Can they trust the social worker to give them clear independent advice?

The role of support groups for grandparent and kinship carers is vital. The Grandparents Group initiated at the Bridge Project in Bradford is an outstanding example of such a group. Its coordinator for 10 years, Mary Womersley, is one of the army of unsung heroes. Her ability to bring together grandparents simply to talk and share with each other has impacted on the many who have attended the group.

For many grandparent carers, there is not simply the need to learn their rights and the responsibilities of their Local Authority: there is also having the opportunity to share their experiences. Many carers feel alone and isolated. Their contemporaries are often working or have shed their child care responsibilities. Carers really benefit from being able to talk to other people in a similar situation. That's why Bridge and similar groups are so vital.

I commend this book. It tells real-life stories of carers who chose to put their own lives on hold so that their loved ones can be properly cared for.

Introduction

Grandparenting: In Adversity and Hope

This book is about our lived experience as grandparents supporting each other, when grandparenting is undertaken in adverse circumstances, far from the usual pattern. Most grandparents complement the efforts of their grown-up children to raise their family by providing practical and moral support – babysitting, collecting children from school, trips to the park, shared Christmas and birthday celebrations, maybe financial help in times of difficulty. By contrast, our grandparents have had to take the grandchildren into their own homes and become substitute parents to them. They have been forced to step in to save them from harm after their adult children have fallen by the wayside due to drug or alcohol addiction. Here we tell our stories about surviving and managing such family catastrophes, with the intention of informing public debate, encouraging good professional practice for those professionals supporting families, and helping others in similar situations.

Whereas 'normal' grandparents are seen in a positive light and generally enjoy their limited responsibilities, grandparents whose children have a history of drug or alcohol dependency often feel blamed as the authors of their own misfortune. As our lives are literally turned upside down, we are often beset by guilt and loneliness, thinking 'What did I do wrong?' and 'Am I the only one?' Finding a self-help group that addressed our anguish, we were able to recover some self-esteem. We were not alone and, in sharing our stories, we came to understand that we had not brought this misfortune on ourselves. We were also able to regain the joy we felt in giving our grandchildren another chance in life and to share accounts of their progress as well as the challenges they presented.

Comparing our stories we could also see wrongs that needed to be righted. Despite the dire situations we faced, we had often received inadequate or poorly focused help that sometimes made our predicaments worse. We uncovered inconsistencies in the way we were treated with regard to financial support or the provision of services. In general we found ourselves part of a hidden problem in society. Here and there we encountered good practice – some exceptional social workers, unexpected routes to assistance, comforting friends and families, clear advice. But this was rare. The chance discovery, by many of us, of a group to support grandparents like us was like an oasis in a desert.

The idea for this book sprang from a Grandparents Group that was started over a decade ago by a worker at the Bridge Project, one of several drug services operating at the time in Bradford in the north of England. Most of us came to The Grandparents Group by way of the Bridge Project, so we knew of its service to substance misusers (our adult children) at first hand. This was a project that had been offering drug treatment in Bradford for over 30 years, with government support and Local Authority funding. Over the years it had expanded from supporting those who were still active substance abusers (with needle exchange, other harm reduction programmes and assistance in detoxifying), to sustaining users in recovery. It helped drug and alcohol users with a whole range of related issues that they face – employment, housing, training and education, criminal behaviour and health support. It supported service users to take responsibility for their actions and to acknowledge the impact these were having on their families and on the local community.

The Grandparents Group was but one of a host of caring activities for which Bridge was renowned. The need continued to be great. In 2015 it was reported in the local press that Bradford District had the worst rate in the county for drug-related deaths – a 15 per cent rise from the previous year. This reflected a larger picture, with the Office for National Statistics reporting a 17 per cent increase in England (2014).

Despite the need, drug education and support have been subject to austerity cuts like many other public services, as can be seen from Chapter 8 in this book, describing Mary Womersley's valiant efforts to set up and run The Grandparents Group. In 2016, following substantial funding cuts, she was offered half-time work or redundancy (though her full-time services were still vitally needed). By 2017, drug services in Bradford had been reorganised under the aegis of a large national charity ('Change, Grow, Live'/cgl). Around a third of the existing staff members were lost. Our Grandparents Group survived, hosted by cgl but now self-managed, without the referral routes to recruit or the links to wider drug services, and with an uncertain future.

Here we tell our individual stories of managing family crises generated by substance abuse. As well as finding each other, we also became aware of the extent to which we are part of a wider picture. There are thousands of grandparents raising their grandchildren in the UK, the majority as a consequence of parental drug use or mental health issues. The exact number is unknown, but most estimates would put it around 100,000.* We are part of an army of 'kinship carers' – the relatives or friends who step in when children cannot be cared for by their parents, for a variety of reasons. Kinship caring is most common in the lowest social class groups, and research studies[1] suggest that three-quarters of kinship carers are impoverished and suffer hardship. The vast proportion of kinship care is 'informal', in the sense that carers have taken on children without a formal court or Social Services contract.

Kinship Caring

Kinship care may be formalised in a variety of ways. Children already looked after by Local Authorities may be fostered with 'family and friends', who are then paid a fostering allowance. They may be placed for adoption with family members, though most adoptions are to strangers.

---

* The data in this paragraph come from a set of very detailed government reports that suggest a lower number, though rising. Most of the figures are estimates and any attempt to clarify the precise number is complicated – first by differing dates, second by variability in the geographical areas covered (England as opposed to the UK, for example), but mostly by the complicated and sometimes overlapping categories applied. Kinship carers are divided into formal and informal categories, with the informal category (164,000 in 2001, according to Nandy et al. 2011, table 3.4, p.21) estimated at 95 per cent of the total. Definitions of 'formal' may vary, in some sources only including Family and Friends foster carers, and not children on Special Guardianship Orders (SGOs) or Residence Orders. Although these three, more formal modes of kinship care are a tiny minority, a precise estimate of the numbers involved is also difficult to find (maybe around 25,000; see Wade et al. 2014). The best estimates would be based on census data, but even studies based on these (e.g. Nandy et al. 2011) yield imprecise results, as do all the calculations about how many are grandparents (the general estimate is around 50 per cent of both formal and informal kinship carers).

Kinship carers who have taken on a child (whether informally or through fostering) may apply to the court for a Residence Order or an SGO (Special Guardianship Order) to strengthen their legal rights vis-à-vis birth parents and to achieve relative autonomy from Social Services. Neither of these orders is as final as an Adoption Order, which transfers parental rights to the adoptive parents. A Residence Order (as of May 2016 renamed a 'Child Arrangements Order') confirms new arrangements for where a child is to live, and bestows parental responsibility on the carer for most decisions about a child's upbringing.[2] An SGO is more secure: the new carer or carers become the child's legal guardians with almost sole parental rights. Only a court can give permission for a birth parent to apply to reverse the Order. Residence Orders and SGOs may be funded through allowances from Local Authorities, but these are generally means-tested and the terms discretionary. All forms of kinship care are on the rise and grandparents constitute around half of such carers, in all categories.

Most of the grandparents in our group had experience of being informal kinship carers who had been propelled into caring for grandchildren full-time in consequence of parental failure to care for the children. Some of the children were already covered by Protection Orders because of the parents' behaviour. By the time we told our stories, all of us had more formalised arrangements. Residence Orders were the most common, but three grandchildren had an SGO and one grandparent had become a 'Family and Friends' foster carer. In some families there was more than one arrangement for different children.

Our group represents a cross-section of society, from those on very modest means, living on state pensions, to fairly comfortable ex-professionals, but with most in the middle. A higher income is no protection against the ravages of drug addiction and alcoholism. All of us had suffered financially in consequence of taking on our grandchildren. Those who were still in work now had to give up; some had paid out thousands in legal fees; and – though they did not count the cost – bringing up children was expensive and ate into savings set aside for retirement.

All of us were now entitled to child benefit, except the foster carer, and some had means-tested child tax credits. One of us had been given an allowance to support a Residence Order, but two others had not. It is clear from our stories that pressure was sometimes put on grandparents to take up Residence Orders, without full explanation of what this meant for their future responsibilities or financial situation. The issue of financial support is also vague for those with SGOs. One of us had an award lasting 2 years, which was then tapered off and stopped, whilst two other grandparents' awards continued. Even taking means testing into account, the logic of these differential payments escaped us, and the whole system seemed inconsistent – not just discretionary, but also arbitrary. However, we know that our situation was usually better than that of most informal kinship carers, who get no financial support at all.

Nationally, around half of grandparents raising grand-children are single parents, predominantly women, divorced or widowed, with an average age in the late 50s. Our group of eight was no different – two were married, but the rest were single women, managing alone. One couple came together and another male ex-partner also joined the group recently, but predominantly this was a group of women. At interview, they range in age from 60 to 77, with an average age of 66, slightly older than the national average of grandparent carers, but perhaps thereby offering a glimpse into the future of grandparents raising grandchildren. Together we seven grandparents were raising 11 children, some in primary and more than half already in secondary school. All of us were white, though not all our children were.[3]

Our circumstances are not atypical then, but as you will see, there are many ways in which families have coped with the double catastrophe of their children turning to substance abuse, and taking on the burden of raising their grandchildren. Each of our stories is different, and they illustrate a range of possible trajectories and outcomes, but there are some common threads. One is our united determination that our grandchildren should not go into care or adoption. When we thought about adoption as an alternative, the sense of family bonds and obligations was paramount. We not only loved our grandchildren, but also 'It was a duty' to care for them and 'You had to protect them'. The thought of them being taken by strangers was unbearable, even to one grandparent who already had adopted children. In this case the first-hand knowledge of how long children wait to be adopted, and how many moves they can have in care before adoption, added to her resistance to this solution.

Comparing Kinship Care to Adoption

Comparing our situation with that of adoptive parents did serve to highlight some notable contrasts and similarities. We did not choose to become parents to our grandchildren, whereas for adoptive parents this is the only motive. Adoptive parents were more like normal parents than we were, in being younger and fitter – and indeed the maximum age gap between parents and adopted children is usually set at around 45 years, which would have prevented some of us from adopting them ourselves had we wished to do so. However, adopted children's circumstances are remarkably similar to our grandchildren's. Both sets of children have suffered parental loss and most have endured a range of traumatic events that have led them to need new parents. Many adopted children these days would have been considered hard to place in the past, given the impact of their damaging early lives. They have a high rate of diagnosed psychiatric disorders, which is shared with those in kinship care and is higher than that found in the general population. A study of children with SGOs showed they had more than double the scores for severe emotional and behavioural problems compared with the general population (see Wade *et al.* 2014).

Our grandchildren had suffered more than most, from violent and neglectful parents with chaotic drug-fuelled lifestyles, which are likely to have impacted on the children even before birth. Most of us were unaware of the traumatic effects of such experience (see p.223 for Caroline Archer's helpful definition of 'trauma'). We knew our children were challenging – indeed this was the stuff of much of our talk in the group – but it was only when we compared the extent of common symptoms of trauma amongst our children that we acknowledged the damage that had been done to them. They displayed a range of quite major signs of emotional and behavioural disorders, such as extreme hyperactivity, poor concentration, rages and tantrums, oppositional behaviour, aggression, difficulties at school, excessive anxiety and so on. In one family all three children had been diagnosed with foetal alcohol spectrum disorder (FASD). We could understand better now that their early damaging experiences had led many of them to develop counter-productive strategies for survival – distancing, asserting control, inability to relinquish control, premature independence, inability to trust, lying, stealing and so on. Most of us were dealing with these consequences of trauma in everyday family life, and several of the parents had tried to access help from Child and Adolescent Mental Health Services (CAMHS) or other bodies. These were very demanding children to care for, not simply children to be rescued, and as grandparents we engaged in a continual struggle to get help for them and to parent them better.

There is one crucial difference between full-time grandparenting and adoption, and that is in our relationship to the birth parents of our children. Adoption generally separates a child from its birth family. Even when contact arrangements are in place they are formalised and tightly controlled. Essentially adoptive parents are protectively distanced from the birth parents of their children. Secretly they may blame the birth parents for the children's problems, though most try not to present the children with a negative picture.

Exactly the opposite happens in our case: we continue to have contact with birth parents – and indeed we feel morally responsible for the behaviour that has led them to being unable to parent. Did we not bring them up? This is a question with which all our grandparents grapple as they try to make sense of why their sons or daughters turned to drugs or alcohol. Not only this: even after we have the grandchildren safe, our adult children are often still living violent, criminal and chaotic lives, or suffering the effects of such lives, and dragging us back into their chaos out of our sense of responsibility for them.

As far as our grandchildren are concerned, this is a matter of concern, as we would like to protect them from all that has gone on before, and offer them a fresh start. It is hard to do this, when their parents continue to make dangerous, threatening or needy intrusions into family life. The only up-side to this situation is that our grandchildren are protected from the fantasy versions of birth parents that many adopted children nurture in their hearts. They may go on caring about their mums and dads, but they have a more realistic and informed view of them. Grandparents also know the background and medical histories of birth parents – they are not dependent on social workers to devise 'narratives' or life story books about the children's pasts, which may be full of half-truths, gaps and comforting formulas.

Barriers to Stability

However, it is not only that our children are continually reminded of their birth parents' inadequacies, or that searing memories of violence and neglect may be revived – even extending to experience of the death or disability of parents through substance abuse. It is also the case that by contrast with the finality of Adoption Orders, the terms of our custodianship over them do not provide sufficient legal protection to challenges from birth parents, who may be subsidised to make claims for access or threats to resume parenting rights.

In our experience this has usually involved birth fathers, who may go to court for access over and over again. Legal challenges to Residence Orders or SGOs have to be investigated and the children are yet again expected to make choices between grandparents and parents, which in practice revives trauma and undermines their security. What we share with adoptive parents in this age of social media is the issue of birth parents approaching our children directly, via Facebook, for example. In our case they may also write to them from prison or send them unwanted gifts or 'loving' cards and letters. This unsolicited contact can be very disturbing to already troubled children and disruptive to family life.

Grandparents have no automatic right to be heard in court, even if they are raising their grandchildren. In family courts they have no right to legal aid and may have to spend thousands on being represented in cases dealing with the safety and future security of their grandchildren. Grandparents with a professional background or wide experience may be able to negotiate their way through, represent themselves in court or find the money to pay the bills, but most grandparents feel lost and fail to mount a legal defence of their position.

When grandparents turn for help to Social Services or other agencies they struggle to get adequate assistance. Academic commentators have for some time noted the lack of qualifying training for social workers in the field of drug and alcohol use, despite this being the backdrop to very many of the social problems with which they must contend. One study highlighted 'an uncomfortable implication... that in relation to welfare outcomes, social workers were not effective in working with families in which there was substance abuse' (See Forrester and Harwin 2008, p.1529). A later work concluded that 'substance abuse played a key role in affecting children's outcomes, yet much of the workforce had little or no training in this area' (Galvani and Thurnham 2012, p.186). Our informal soundings amongst professionals in this field and in health suggest that the situation has not improved, and that there is an urgent need for more focused training.

Our stories provide numerous examples of what it feels like to be in dire need but not to get informed and understanding responses. We are well aware that social workers are under immense pressure, with excessive workloads and unrealistic expectations of what they can deliver, but what we experience is a failure to see us as partners in keeping children safe and happy (and in the process saving the state resources and time). We are sometimes denied information that we need in order to parent our grandchildren, on the grounds of 'confidentiality'. Or the options for achieving security for the children are not sufficiently explained to us, if at all. Some of us experience a cavalier lack of assessment of our needs and circumstances (as when the grandchildren are more or less dumped on our doorsteps), whilst others are held up to intense and paralysing scrutiny. Many of us feel blamed. Decisions about removing children from their birth parents often seem arbitrary from our perspective: grandparents who report serious concerns about the neglect or chaotic circumstances in which their substance-abusing children are bringing up their own children are often dismissed or ignored, whilst in other cases children are removed summarily and without any opportunity for interventions to help the parent(s).

There are always exceptions – social workers who go the extra mile and who are advocates for us to get the support we need. One of us has acknowledged that the only way to access the services she needs for her disabled children is to remain as a Family and Friends foster carer, though her bid to do this was initially resisted. Schools on the whole have listened and some have provided remarkable back-up when our grandchildren are displaying signs of disturbance or anxiety. School nurses and solicitors have guided us. However, it is only since April 2016 that Special Guardians have been made eligible for the Adoption Support Fund, which helps adoptive parents to access therapeutic help for their children and the financial support to cover it (see Stevenson 2015); and this right does not extend to those with Residence Orders or informal carers.

Self-Help Support Groups

This is why The Grandparents Group has proved such a lifeline to many of us, allowing us to compare notes, access information and explore solutions. The coordinator also acted on occasion as an advocate with authorities, trying to get a better deal or a breakthrough, supporting us to go to court or simply offering a listening ear. The group works because it is independent of the authorities – it is not run by Social Services or other public agencies, so members feel free to speak of their predicaments without fear of the consequences. Because the coordinator had personal experience of the issues faced by members, and had built up long-standing relations with them, she was trusted. The group has survived her unwilling departure because of the deepening relationships its members have developed with each other – as one put it: 'It has become like family.'

All of us have made sacrifices to look after our grandchildren, but on the whole we feel enriched by the experience. Being forced to give up paid work has led to social isolation as well as loss of income and status in society, but we have begun to create new networks around our new purpose in life – with schools and playgroups, through organising activities to keep our children happy and fulfilled, and seeking the help and support they need to address challenging or disturbed behaviour. We now look forward rather than back, delighting in our children's progress, proud of their every step towards maturity and comforted by the knowledge that they need us. We have become resilient and resourceful in fighting for them, coping with everyday stresses and still managing to maintain some contact with their parents. At least one parent has been able to come off drugs and resume parenting her children; though without considerable child caring by grandparents this would have been unlikely.

We have a couple of major anxieties. One is the prospect of adolescent upheavals, with our first-hand knowledge of how our children first went off the rails at this point and how powerless we had been to prevent them sinking into addiction and all that goes with it. So far, the fears of history repeating itself have not been borne out, but we cannot take it for granted.

Our second fear, as much older parents and with many of us single, is that our grandchildren may have to face our deaths or incapacitating illness at some key point in their development. Who can be found to substitute for us if this happens? It is too great a responsibility to easily shift onto anyone else's shoulders, especially as our grandchildren will still need more than ordinary support to launch them into independence. It is hard for us to ask anyone to take it on – indeed mostly impossible – and we are unclear how the children are to be protected in this contingency. What is surprising and reassuring, however, is that whilst we all suffer some of the disabilities of age, the need to keep moving and active because of the children has pushed us to better health and resilience.

There is little recognition of the important role we play after the rising social tide of drug and alcohol dependency has left so many victims in its wake. If we and thousands of other grandparents did not step in as substitute parents, the number of children in care (already breaking records) would swell dramatically.

We are aware that keeping a child in public care is very expensive. The most recent estimates from the National Audit Office (2014) calculate over £30,000 per annum for a child in foster care and considerably more for a child in residential care (more than £130,000). Kinship carers, even those with formalised orders, look after children for a fraction of this cost. Kinship carers without formal orders or a fostering allowance come free to the state, and we know their number is much greater than those currently recognised. We argue that we offer these children close and familial security, with some chance at least of easing the traumatic start they had in life and protecting against disturbed or even criminal futures.

What we need, however, is a level playing field compared to other carers for traumatised children. We need therapeutic services as much as adopted children; it is not unreasonable to suggest that we should be able to access financial support that is more than 'discretionary' and which recognises that we have taken on a full-time job as carers, which will stretch us to the limits as we grow older. We therefore support a statutory entitlement to financial help for kinship carers. We need social workers and other public officers to be adequately trained in the effects of substance misuse. We need to be believed when we report abuse. We need occasional respite – even a free babysitting service would allow some of us to enjoy a social life. It would help if we had access to some safe back-up in times of need such as illness. More legal protection and support is required to keep the children safe from birth parents still intent on putting their own needs before the security of their children. We hope that our accounts of living through the tsunami of taking on our grandchildren will give pause for thought – and lead to action.

A Note from the Editor About How We Put This Book Together

The inspiration for our book goes back to a point at which we realised how little is known or understood about the contribution we make to services for substance users. Some of us had already been involved in campaigning activities in a small way and benefited from communication with organisations like Grandparents Plus and the Family Rights Group. Some of us had also been interviewed by the media (see Mary Womersley's account in Chapter 8). But in a bid to address misunderstandings and to expose the hidden army of grandparent carers, we determined to tell our stories. The book is based on eight lengthy interviews, which were transcribed and then edited down into chapters. We have used pseudonyms to protect the identity of those involved. Our diversity in socioeconomic as well as geographic backgrounds is reflected in the way we express ourselves through Yorkshire idioms and turns of phrase. It is unusual for such a range of voices to be heard and the experience of 'ordinary' people is often buried. As one of us says, 'Because we were upset and we were stunned by it all we said nothing'. This book represents a bid to break the silences and tell the inside story of grandparenting in adversity.

We are deeply indebted to Caroline Archer, who read the manuscript and wrote an Afterword, helping grandparents to understand the impact of parental substance use on children's development.

We must also acknowledge a debt of gratitude to the Bridge Project in Bradford, for initiating and supporting our self-help group for over nearly a decade; and to Pat Caplan, Lionel Caplan, Russell Murray and Sara Cooper for believing in our project as a necessary and important intervention and for reading drafts of the book and making suggestions for improvement.

Notes

1. These are based on work carried out at the University of Bristol (Nandy *et al.* 2011; Selwyn *et al.* 2014), and backed up by research done by the Family Rights Group, cited widely in the press (e.g. *The Independent*, 13 October 2015).

2. The change of name does not affect the terms, and since 'Residence Order' is the term used by members of The Grandparents Group, it has not been changed in the following chapters. Some grandparents, struggling with the jargon of an unfamiliar system, call it a 'Residency Order'.

3. Two-thirds of all children living in kinship care are white, but the second-biggest category is made up of Asian children (Nandy *et al.* 2011, table 3.4, p.21). In Bradford there is a large Asian population and consequently a sizeable proportion in kinship care. However, we think that many of these may be grandparents and other relatives co-parenting children in multi-generational households and thereby part of a different social phenomenon.

References

Forrester, D. and Harwin, J. (2008) 'Parental substance misuse and child welfare: Outcomes for children two years after referral.' *British Journal of Social Work 38*, 1518–1535.

Galvani, S. and Thurnham, A. (2012) 'Substance abuse.' In M. Davies (ed.) *Social Work with Adults*. Basingstoke, UK: Palgrave Macmillan.

Glaser, K., Montserrat, E., Waginger, U., Price, D., Stuchbury, R. and Tinker, A. (2010) *Grandparenting in Europe*. London: Grandparents Plus and King's College, London. A useful comparative overview of policy and practice in the UK, Europe and the USA.

Nandy, S., Selwyn, J., Farmer, E. and Vaisey, P. (2011) *Spotlight on Kinship Care: Using Census Microdata to Examine the Extent and Nature of Kinship Care at the Turn of the Twentieth Century*. Research report. Bristol, UK: University of Bristol.

National Audit Office (2014) *Children in Care*. Accessed on 22/11/17 at www.nao.org.uk/report/children-in-care.

Office for National Statistics (2014) *Deaths Related to Drug Poisoning in England and Wales*. Statistical bulletin. London: ONS.

Selwyn, J., Wijedasa, D. and Meakings, S. (2014) *Beyond the Adoption Order: Challenges, Intervention, Disruption*. Bristol, UK: Hadley Centre for Adoption and Foster Care Studies, School of Policy Studies, University of Bristol.

Stevenson, L. (2015) *Special Guardianship Orders: What Needs to Change? Community Care*. Accessed on 18/9/18 at www.communitycare.co.uk/2015/09/24/specialguardianships.

Wade, J., Sinclair, I. and Stuttard, L. (2014) *Investigating Special Guardianship: Experiences, Challenges and Outcomes*. York, UK: Social Policy Research Unit, University of York.

1

Jane

'Trying to bring 'em up right'

Jane (69) and her husband Harry found themselves looking after their two grandchildren, William (4) and James (nearly 2), after their son Ian and his wife, both alcoholics, had neglected and hurt them.

* * *

It was late on a Saturday afternoon when we had a phone call from the police, telling us that my son and daughter-in-law had been arrested, and would we look after the children for the weekend? James had been injured. He'd been bruised all over. The social workers brought the children and they arrived with a bag of clothes on the doorstep. No nappies, no milk. Two little tots, very frightened. James was just before his second birthday and William was 4. And they just arrived on the doorstep and we had to run round to the shops and get some stuff for 'em. We'd no beds for them. We doubled up. My husband Harry went into bed with James in the double bed in the back bedroom. I had a folding-out couch and me and William got in there.

It was a shock, but we knew that there'd been something going on. We knew who'd done it. We knew Mum had done it because she had lots of convictions against her for grievous bodily harm – things she'd done before she met my son, Ian. And then of course there was all the domestic violence, because she was a very violent person. But Ian just put up with it. And you see...they were both drinkers. So alcohol came into it as well. So we were very fearful for these children anyway. We always used to be very fearful, what was going on down at their house. We used to take 'em out at weekends but because we were both working they'd never been here to sleep. When he was only 3 William used to come and say, 'I like to come here because I get peace and quiet.'

Getting them full-time was a great shock. My husband had been retired a week. We just had a week when he were retired. We think she planned it so that we could look after these children, because she'd said in the past she didn't want the boys. She wanted rid of them. And the Social Services knew all about her. We were devastated. We were just retiring, and going to have a retirement life together. I worked in an electronics factory, and Harry were a builder. He worked outdoors all t'time – he had a hard job. And he was looking forward to retirement. Now we literally had to turn our lives around. We were like young parents again – but not young parents, because we were both in our 60s. I was 61 – I'd just retired as well. And Harry took an early retirement: he was 64.

The police came as well as social workers, and they sent a photographer the day after they arrived and he stood James up and photographed him. And then, a few days after, we had to take him up to the infirmary and he had to be x-rayed all over his body. And he screamed and screamed and screamed. I had to go in, put a jacket on, hold him down. And they even did his fingers to see if he'd any broken bones, but he didn't. This was for if there was going to be a case against the parents.

In the meantime my son was still in custody. They kept him in for 3 days and grilled him and grilled him and said if he didn't plead guilty then he'd have to go to jail. And unfortunately the night it happened, he was drunk. He hadn't a clear head, right. He hadn't got a clear mind, so, he couldn't remember, really, what had happened. So he pleaded guilty when he shouldn't have pleaded guilty. They held her at first and then they let her out. So she got off with it. But she was a very cunning person and she would have talked her way out of it anyway. After they had William, my son tried to protect him. And then when she had James, she was very violent still, and Social Services had to call my son out of work and he had to come home and care for them, 24 hours. He had to be their full-time carer, so as he could keep her away from them a little bit. After he'd to give his job up to look after the children, he turned more to drink then.

We turned our heads around – and people were very good, gave us all sorts of stuff, yer know, toys, clothes, everything. They came and helped us. Social Services were quite good at first; they brought us two beds. But when they left them that day they asked us to sign a little bit of paper. And they said you can go to the court on Monday and you can get a Residence Order. And we had no idea what a Residence Order meant! In the meantime, they said, if she [their mother] turns up at the house, you phone the police. We were told to go down to the magistrates' court. There must have been a bit of a hearing – I can't remember what happened now. I remember we just filled a form in. And then Social Services said we'll pay for this Residence Order. At that time we just thought it was going to be like, a few days, maybe a couple of weeks, while everything settled down, and everything was sorted out. But then afterwards there was a meeting at our house. The social worker came, a key worker came, about four people came. And they were all saying, 'We're really sorry' and sympathising with us, which we couldn't understand. Then they said, 'Well, you do realise that it will not be just a short-term thing – if you've signed a Residence Order it will be a long-term thing, at least until they're 16.' Well that was an almighty blow! We didn't realise that it meant that. We felt trapped. But then you can't feel trapped for too long because there's two children that are so nervous, so scared, that have had an awful upbringing so far, that you've got to turn it round, and say right, then we'll give you a better life than what you've had already. These two poor children, they need somebody, you know. So, that's it.

There was no kind of assessment, nobody checked us out. They only knew us, because – and I've just remembered this – the boys were put on a Child Protection Register after Ian gave up work to look after 'em full-time. Then there were [Social Services] meetings and I used to go – there'd be a policeman there; there'd be a school teacher there; all sat round the table. Everyone'd give a little report and if I thought their mum were doing anything wrong, I'd say in my report. She were there, too, and she'd fly off the handle, and we'd have a bit of swearing, and then they'd realise what she were really like. I do remember once, social workers there, saying to me, 'What would you do, right...' – I think they were grilling me then – 'What would you do if the children had to come to live with you? Would you be able to do it?' I remember saying, 'Yeah, well, we'd have to do, wouldn't we? If it were needed.'

But when they originally brought these children to us, they didn't know really, what sort of people we were. We could have been anybody. Nobody looked round our house.

And the children's social worker was more sympathetic towards the mother. She said, you know, 'What an awful thing it is for a mother to lose a child.' And I turned round and I said, 'No, you don't know her.' The other social worker had just left and this one was a brand new worker who didn't know *anything* about their background. And I said, 'You don't know their mum. She'll be quite happy now because she's like a free woman again!' For a while they thought that Ian had done it and he was the bad one. This was in August. September it went to the magistrates' court. Ian was very, very scared that he was going to be put in prison. Although his wife went to court too, they didn't even ask her any questions. But by now they'd read all the notes about her previous convictions and they realised what she was like. So Ian got community hours to do and a suspended 2-year sentence. And he did it all. He did everything he should do. But then – he went back to her. So that caused a problem here.

They said we were entitled to child benefit and tax credits. I had to fill all these forms in. But their mum was still claiming, while the children were living here! For 8 months there was a confusion because we tried to claim and she were claiming. Then it had to be proved that we were looking after them and the social worker used to come about every month or so to check. So then their mum was in trouble, she got into trouble for that and got fined for that and they took all the money back. At first that was all the money we had. We'd no money because I'd got made redundant, and we decided to retire together. We could probably manage on the bit o' money we had. I got the pension; he didn't. There was to be no pension for him till he was going to be 65. And then we got these two children! Social Services just presumed that we could manage. And because we were upset and we were, you know, stunned by it all, we said nothing.

We could not have let the children go anywhere else. These poor children – you know, you couldn't say, 'Well no, sorry, but we can't have 'em.'

Settling In

Their parents did get access; they got two days a week. Social Services were not involved. They didn't really want to know by that time. Because they'd got this Residence Order, it were left up to us then. We used to take the boys to the park in Shipley. Their mum wasn't allowed to come up here. My son could come any time he wanted, which shows you he wasn't seen as guilty as her. And she missed more times than what she came.

They settled in quite well with us. But at first James, who were just under 2, could not speak a word. All he did were scream for everything. Just screamed. He couldn't even say, 'Ta', 'Hello' – you know, anything. And William was very, very scared. Anytime anybody banged a door, or they heard a police car outside on the main road, they'd both cower. William were frightened to death. Anybody who came to the door, anybody who came to the house – he'd hide at the back of the settee. From his past experience, he'd know that somebody knocking on the door would probably be a policeman, arresting them. His mum were always getting Ian into trouble and having him arrested. And it were his daddy, and he loved his daddy. He were a very, very frightened little boy.

And then of course he had to start school in the September. He'd only been here for a month. We had to go and buy all the uniform. We'd to sort all the schooling out. And for about a month, every day, he cried, going to school. Would we be picking him up? Would we be leaving him there? Would we be coming back for him? He was so frightened, so frightened. And when we used to bring him home from school, because his mum and dad didn't feed him properly, he'd say, 'What can I have before me dinner comes out? What can I have before me dinner comes out?' And he used to drive us absolutely crazy. And we couldn't understand why he said that, but afterwards we realised that probably before, when he got home from nursery, he didn't get anything till maybe 8 o'clock at night. They'd no routines. You know, they'd put them to bed, 10, 11 o'clock, whenever they fancied it. And she would shout all the time, you see, every night. Ian did all t'cooking. He did all t'washing. He were like, the mainstay in the house.

James was already going to the nursery so we kept him on there for 2, 3 days a week. We kept him as normal as we could do. We had to pay for that, but it meant we could have a bit of time to ourselves in the day. We'd just retired, and it were a huge sacrifice – and a huge thing that we'd taken on. And we'd never get any time together. William went to school and he was full-time when he went. So we did get a little bit of time then to ourselves. We could nip out, fast as we could, we'd nip somewhere, have a couple of hours out, you know, by the time James came out at dinnertime. Nursery was very good – they used to give him a dinner for free, so we didn't have to get back while 1 o'clock. So in 4 hours we could do all sorts.

We carried on doing this, and then came the second September. William moved up into Year 1, and James started at that school in the nursery. School were very good again, and for a couple of days a week they let James go to nursery in the morning and to lunch club and crèche in the afternoon. So for 2 days a week then, we had a full day, from 9 o'clock till 3. And then December came and Harry died.

It was just 16 months after they came – we'd gone out for the day to Harrogate. We'd been in the park but Harry didn't look right well. When we got back to the car he couldn't lift James up into the car, which was most unusual, because he were a big, strong man. He drove the car and we stopped at a Co-op shop on the way back. He got out, went to get some milk for us – and collapsed in the shop, and died. Very suddenly – he had a massive heart attack.

We were sat in the car waiting for him and thinking there must be a big queue. And then William saw an ambulance at t'back of us. 'I hope it's not my grandad', he said. And I said, 'Well, I hope it isn't.' And we sat, watching. And then, you know, your heart starts beating fast and I were waiting and waiting – and when they opened the doors, I saw it were Harry on the stretcher. So I opened the car door, ran to see him and then got the boys and ran back. The ambulance lady said, 'I'm sorry but we've got to go.' We were stood on the pavement, just watching. A man came up to me, and he said, 'Are you okay?' 'No', I said, 'They've just taken my husband away.' 'Right', he said, 'I'm an off-duty policeman, I'll help you.' I said to him, 'I can't even lock the car door. I don't even know how to lock the door.' You know, I'd never drove. So he locked the door for us, left it outside this Co-op, and very kindly took us to the hospital in his car. We got to the hospital and they took us into a side room. James were sat with me. They took William out into another room with the nurses. And then they just said, 'You know, it's not looking good.' And then they came and said he'd died. I think he might already have been dead when we arrived there. It were just like that. And it were just such a bolt out of the blue.

So then we'd a funeral to arrange. Both the boys were confused, didn't know where Grandad was. I couldn't explain to James – he just thought he was in an ambulance, for months afterwards. William was the most confused, couldn't understand, you know, where he'd gone. We tried to explain to him, but of course you can't.

The funeral were the day before Christmas Eve. A terrible time but people rallied round. My sister-in-law stepped in, said come to us for Christmas dinner; you're not doing it yourself. The family – presents were arriving, from everybody! Never seen presents arrive, like they did that year. Even from neighbours that I've never spoke to before. So we got over Christmas and I took 'em straight back to school. Kept life as normal as what I could do. Just rallied on. And Social Services did pay for some taxis to get me down to school and back, because I can't drive. I said to 'em – 'I'm stuck' – they knew then about Harry. But that only lasted a few months and then they expected me to manage.

I tried then for a Residence Order allowance, but didn't get that for, oh, a good couple of years after Harry died. It makes an awful lot of difference – pays for taxis, you know, pays for school trips, pays for lots and lots of things. And I had such good friends and neighbours that were very, very good to me. School were absolutely excellent. And you just, like, get on with it then. But I were on my own with them now and that were different, that were like a new situation. One only 3 year old, one were 5, so you can imagine – they were fighting all the time and I couldn't leave them on their own. Getting used to it were really hard. And of course being on me own as well, losing Harry as well you see, after 41 years we'd been married. I'd lost so much. But then of course I've gained these two and they're a great comfort to me.

Living with Grandchildren

Eight years they've been here now. They're very good at school, very well behaved at school. James had problems sitting still, you know, listening, concentrating – it's taken about 2 years, maybe 3 years to learn how to sit down at school. He's very hyperactive is James. William has always been the quiet, frightened one, because of his past, what he's seen, the violence. James didn't remember much about it. But he doesn't like dark places. Now whether she shoved him in a dark room... He doesn't like noises, doesn't like noisy things – there'd be a lot of banging and clattering going on when they were little.

Now, they do sort of normal things, they play out, they can interact with other children. I should say they're quite well-balanced boys. They sometimes ask why they live with me and I say it was because their mum and dad couldn't look after them. William knew why, because he could remember his mum's disruptions and violence towards them, and said he was glad he lived with me. Their friends at school have asked if their mum and dad were dead, and they have just answered that they live with Grandma and left it at that.

But we still have the problems. I still have, like, this aggression – there's a lot of aggression from William...anger. He's not angry at school – he's angry with me. He turns it against me. And now their dad has sort of deserted 'em, and rarely comes, except for birthdays and Christmas, I think they're angry about that as well. My son's let us down big time. And he keeps letting us down. He'll tell them he's coming, and he doesn't come, which to children is a big, big disappointment. So it's even worse, you see. And he only lives down the road. So there is still this anger problem – maybe William thinks I've told his dad not to come – I don't know. He knows I haven't done that, but maybe in his mind, he maybe blames me for something – I don't know. But he knows I'm not going to fall out with him, whatever he does – and he's always sorry afterwards. But I sometimes have to take things off of him. You know, like a consequence. I've got to have a bit of control or they're going to take over my life aren't they? It's trying to get the balance between being mean and being too soft.

The Social Services have finished with me now. Unless anything really important flies out, I'm completely off their books. Which is a bit scary, because sometimes you need a bit of a back-up. I've had to keep going. I'm such a positive person, that tries to keep going anyway. I tend just to get on with life and try not to let things upset me. I have had a couple of health issues – I lost quite a bit of weight when Harry died – but nothing too major, which is a good thing, because if we'd anything major, I don't know what we'd do. I still walk a lot. I've had to carve a new life for meself. I go out, but only through the day, you know, when they're at school. I go bowling, and I go on a walking group, and to a history group. They only involve a couple of hours a day, but it's a bit of 'me-time'. Otherwise I think I'd go completely up the wall. Never go out at night. If you do you've got to get babysitters – and it's expensive. My family would do it, but I've just got into the habit now of not going out on a night. I find it easier just to go out through the day. And I go out with the boys at weekends and we go out in the holidays.

But I do get tired on a night. Your life's taken up with doing school things, organising on a night when they've gone to bed. It's the same routine every single night. But if we didn't have a routine, everything would go to pot. After they come back from school, we have tea, then we play out a little bit, or we play inside. Then we get bathed, then we do homework, we do reading. One goes to bed an hour earlier than the other, so I can try and get them to sleep. And then you start packing lunches up, you start getting school clothes, you're getting the football gear ready for next morning. And by t'time you've done, you look at your clock and it's nearly 10 o'clock! And then you think, it'll all start again at half past seven!

Sometimes it's been really fraught – William used to wake James up every night. So that's been a major crisis.

They used to be in the same bedroom, and it's worked, for years, because they liked each other's company – they felt safe with each other. And then William started to get a little bit awkward. It's like it were a bit of attention-seeking – because he's doing this, I'm having to go see to him, aren't I? He were just trying my patience. Whether it were because he's growing up, you know, and we're going to have this trouble, I don't know. I mean he's not a teenager yet! But then I decided to separate them at night and use the box room for a bedroom for William, and sleeping arrangements have got rather good now.

The most difficult part of having them is when they start fighting, or when they start being a little bit rude to me. If we go out and they're awkward – you know, if they stamp their feet and have tantrums. And people think, 'Oh look at that grandma there, she can't control them children.' And they don't realise that you're looking after 'em all the time. Or they'll come up to you on the bus and they'll say, 'Have you got 'em for t'day? What time are they going back to their mum and dad?' And then they'll look at me, will t'boys, and we'll just look at each other, and we'll just smile, you know. And sometimes I'll say, 'No, they live with me', or sometimes we don't even bother. If we don't know the people, we just let it go.

At first, the fact that there were two of them made it difficult, because they wouldn't share. Somebody gave us a bubble car in the garden, and it were nearly like World War III! Then the girl next door passed one of theirs over, so that they could have one each. But now it's worked out a bit better. And sometimes I think it's nice because they've got each other to play with. Sometimes they'll get a game out, or something, or they'll get the cars out – whatever we're doing, they'll do it together. They'll get the lorries out – we've got

Eddie Stobart, we've got boxes and boxes of toys. And they'll play together.

Reflections on Getting Old

I think the most difficult thing is my age. My age, I think, is against me. I wish I could be 20 years younger than what I am now. I think it's quite daunting for them to think, 'Oh, Grandma's old' – and me to think, 'I'm getting older.' And me, thinking, 'I hope I can carry on like this for years and years to come.' Sometimes you'll meet your friends and they'll go, 'Do you know, I've just booked a cruise!' And you'll think, 'Well, how lucky!' But then I think, 'Well no, some people that are on their own are very lonely. At least you're not lonely. At least you've got the company – and you take 'em out, and you enjoy what you do.'

I take them out to interesting places, so that it's a bit interesting for me too. We went to York last week to the Railway Museum, and they love it. We go there a lot. I sometimes take 'em to educational places, where we can all learn something. I like doing that. I like teaching 'em. I want to give 'em a bit of knowledge. That's my idea. My mum and dad gave me knowledge. Didn't have any money; both mill workers. But me dad had a lot of knowledge – what I'd call useless information, but not that useless. Sometimes in a pub quiz, that useless information used to win me a question!

What makes me happy is laughing, you know, playing with 'em in t'garden, having a game of badminton, taking them to t'theatre, taking them to museums and taking them on railway journeys. Getting excited – meself as well, you know – about whether we might be catching the train that goes through to Edinburgh. 'Are we getting on that train, Grandma? We won't be getting on t'rubbish one – will we be getting on t'TransPennine, Grandma, or will we be getting

CrossCountry?' And I'm saying 'Well, it depends what train comes in first.' You know, taking 'em out. Being with 'em. Funnily enough, being down in that school playground, having a laugh with the mums. You know, still being able to chat with everybody. It brings you into touch with a lot of younger people who I've palled up with and we sometimes meet up, in the park, or at the Funtime Play Centre. And when it's school holidays, the children come on the walking club with me. Last week they came with me and we did a sculpture trail in Shipley, on the canal and the river bank. This time I thought – let James carry the leaflet, not William – because William sort of, takes over a bit sometimes with James. All the walkers were shouting, 'Right James, what's coming up next?'

I think it's quite a nice experience with grandchildren. It's like a spin-off, in't it, from your children? But it's quite nice, because you've been allowed to have a bit more time with children. That's how I look at it. It's given me something to focus on. You know, something to get up for in a morning.

Looking to the Future and Trying to Make Sense of the Past

Nobody ever suggested fostering or adoption – and anyway, there was no question. I'd a just said, 'No. No, no way. They're stopping wi' me.' Somebody did say to me a few years ago, when Harry were alive – she said, '*I* wouldn't take 'em on. Oh no, no, no – get 'em adopted.' And we said, 'Nooo, no, no, no, they're our grandchildren, they're our children, and you know, they're part of our family. No.' And I often think, I wonder what she'd have done in that situation. You don't know, when you're in that situation, what you would do. But I know definitely. *No!* Nobody's having 'em. No, not even when Harry died. There was no question of it, you know. I knew that I could – I knew somehow that I would get through it, keep going. And they kept me going.

But you know what? Ian did have more children. Even before Harry died there was another child due, and we were visited and asked to take it. We said, 'You must be joking!' That was a little girl and my niece took her, so we do see her. Then there was another boy – and he did get adopted and we haven't seen him since, though we do have a photo of him that I look at with the boys. Both the children had medical problems. I think losing these children hurt me more than Ian, but we just had to accept it. She had no more then.

There's no chance that the boys could go back to their parents – no chance their mum could have 'em, definitely not. Maybe my son – if he framed his self. That's a Yorkshire saying, in't it? But he's not doing it. He's obviously enjoying being with her – it's what he's done, he's chosen his wife over his children. He'd prefer to be with her than to come and sit down and help me with them. It wouldn't be a case of him having to do anything if he came, just him playing with them. At certain times, you just physically can't be with them. You're washing up, or you're making beds upstairs or something. And you don't know what they're doing down here. It's difficult, bringing these children up on my own.

Thinking back to when my own children were young – I have Ian and a daughter, Angela. As far as I know they were just normal children. They did normal things. We took Ian for years to play football, and Angela, she played music. We took 'em on holiday, took 'em out at weekends. You know, did just normal things. But then when Ian were about 16, one day we found half a bottle of wine that had gone. We used to get stuff in for Christmas, and you'd find some of it were missing out of the bottle. Harry at one time liked a lager, and we'd find a lager might be missing. And this led to Ian going out drinking. When he were old enough, he went out drinking and caused quite a few problems. He was a weekend drinker, like a binge drinker, destructive at the weekends. As he got older he would come in drunk, and then you'd be wondering, 'Is he putting the gas oven on? Is he cooking pizzas? What's he doing?' – you know – 'Are we going to have the house on fire?' It got to be a problem. And then of course, he's always in the pub now.

People'll think, won't they, 'What sort of an upbringing did he have?' But he had a normal upbringing. They'll think he's an awful person. But he's not really an awful person, he is a quite nice person, deep down, it's just his drink spoils him. People don't say it to your face, they just say, 'I've just seen your Ian and he's been absolutely legless.' And I'll say, 'Well, thanks for telling me.' I'm thinking, 'Well, yeah, but he wan't brought up like that.' That's what you try and say to 'em. I mean, we weren't drinkers. The back end of Harry's life, we stopped drinking altogether. He just said, 'Right, no more, I don't want any more lager', you know. We didn't go out that often anyway.

But when you get a son who's a drinker, it spoils the atmosphere. It spoils the parties, it ruins the families, it ruins everything. It's not just them it ruins; it ruins the whole spectrum, because you're afraid to be in their company, in case they show theirselves up, in case they come in absolutely... sloshed. It does have a big effect. And William has seen him drinking, you see, so he'll say, now – he's quite old-fashioned – 'We don't like beer, do we, Grandma? No. No, we don't. And we definitely don't like wine, do we?' I don't have any drink in this house at all. But you see, I had a grandad who was an alcoholic. So whether that was anything to do with it, I don't know; whether it's genetic... I think it's just social drinking that went out of hand. Because Ian didn't have a girlfriend while he were older, he was free – and so he'd just get drunk all the time. It's definitely his downfall. It could affect his liver eventually. And you can't protect the boys all their life. They are at some point of life going to try alcohol. I know that they're going to do it. But you just hope that they don't go down the path that their dad went down.

Ian met up with the boys' mum 11 years ago. She was very charming; he brought her up to the house to meet us. He were 30 when he met her and she were 23, something like that. I knew there was something a little bit different about her, but I didn't know she'd all these convictions – that had happened before he met her. I think she'd had a bit of a rough life to start off with and I think she must just have gone off the rails. We found out she was *very* well-known at the police station. They all knew her. Ian got caught up with her, fell in love with her, and then she became pregnant, straight away. And then she said, 'Well, if you don't marry me, you won't see the baby.' So she conned him – trapped him into it. And it went from there, and it just got worse and worse. We realised that she wasn't doing things right with William – and Ian'd come up here and he'd have black eyes – she used to hit him all the time.

Now I don't have anything to do with her. After Harry died I said, 'Well I'm not bringing 'em to t'park – not on my own.' Cos I couldn't drive, I couldn't take the scooters and stuff, so I said, 'Right, I'll meet you up in Westover Park instead.' And she only came about twice and then she never came again. So they don't see her – they've not seen her now for years. William mentioned her, the other day. Somebody was shouting outside, which is very unusual, shouting at her children, and she was swearing. And he came running in, did William, and he said, 'Did you hear that?' and I said, 'Yeah', and he said, 'She were effing at them, Grandma.' And he said, 'That's what me mum used to do.' He's never said that before. 'Yeah', he said, 'She used to shout right loud at us, like that.' It must have stirred him up a bit when he heard it. He still doesn't like…they don't like violence on t'television. They don't like anybody arguing – they don't like it. They get really frightened if anybody starts arguing.

Compared to my own children I think I'm more protective with these two, because of course, there were two of us then looking after 'em then. Now it's just me, and what happens if I'm gone before they grow up? I presume they would be looked after for me, probably by my daughter. I'm sure she would. She's the type of person that would. I haven't approached her yet, because, well, you don't want to put a burden on somebody else, do you? Because we knew how it felt to have them put on us. You know, it's a feeling of dread – that we're responsible now for these two children. We've done our bit and we've got it again. Thinking, 'Will we be able to do it? Will we be able to cope with it? Will we be able to manage these two children?'

Support and the Grandparents' Group

I were told about The Grandparents Group by the school nurse – she must have known Mary [the coordinator]. That was very, very lucky, because I wouldn't have known otherwise. There's nothing advertised, for a Grandparents Group in Bradford. The group was more or less a godsend to me. Me and Harry were going to go together. Mary was going to come and interview us in the November, but she was poorly and she never came. And then the month after, Harry died. Mary came to see me in the January. And she came a couple of times, and then she said, 'Right, do you think you'd like to come?' And it were in the March when I went. And it was the scariest thing I've ever done, even though, you know, I can talk! Sometimes I get really, really nervous about meeting new people. I didn't know what I was going to find or what I was going to talk about.

Amelia was there – and a couple of others came – erm... Lucy and her sister, and I don't know whether Molly were there or not. But there were just a few of us in that little room and it were really nice, and I quite enjoyed it. I told me story and I cried, and they all cried – because it was still very raw, was Harry's death. But since then I do not like missing it. And I've made more friends – you know I've got lots more friends – and the children have got friends, you know. We go out and mix a little bit – you know, like the picnic and the Christmas party.

I do have other support as well. My daughter, she's very good. And after Harry died I did have a support carer, who came every fortnight. And then it got to be once a month. It was the school nurse again – she said, 'Jane, why don't you have a little bit of help?' She got in touch with Social Services and they said, 'Right then, she can have some support care on a Sunday.' Sundays can be very long. So the boys used to go for 6 hours on a Sunday, which was wonderful. They were only little, and they were really well behaved and she used to take them out to the park. And they used to play on her Wii – because, you know, I didn't have one – so they used to play on all her electrical stuff. And they used to like that. They only do the support normally for 9 months, but because of my circumstances, I think they felt a bit sorry for me. So they extended it. And it actually extended to 3 years, which was really good. And then it just stopped. But now, because they're older, we do other things on a Sunday, so it doesn't matter so much.

Me sister-in-law goes to church at Idle. Now we used to go and have dinner down there once a month on a Saturday. They enjoyed doing that as well. But now they go swimming on a Saturday dinner time so we've had to knock that one –

you know, you can't do everything. They go for a swimming lesson on a Saturday and this [Residence Order] allowance allows me to pay for that, you see. But you have to reapply, every year.

Reflecting on Events

I think if you're a grandparent looking after grandchildren, you've got to go back and pretend you're a parent. And you've got to put some discipline in, because they're not like grandchildren. You've got to pretend that they're your children again. And that they can't get away with everything. And you can't give 'em everything they want. You know, like grandparents would do, spoil 'em for t'day, take them out, buy 'em bags of sweets and that – no, you can't do that. Because you've taken over that other role, haven't you? My best friend has got two boys – her grandchildren, same age as these two. I went away with her for a weekend last year, to Windsor and London. We went on a coach trip – she went with her two and I went with my two. And when we got back, she said she were exhausted! And she said, 'Jane! I'll take me hat off to you, I don't know how you do it.' She said, 'They were much better behaved than these two of mine, and I'm glad that they're going back home to their parents tonight.' She were running up and down t'bus – they wouldn't sit still!

In fact I get a lot of praise. 'You need a medal, Jane, you need a medal.' Everybody says, 'I don't know how you do it, because I've had mine for a day and I'm exhausted.' But I think it's the routines, if you can keep it going. Luckily – touch wood – I'm not often poorly. I'm not often ill, but that's the fear I have. That if I were taken into hospital or anything like that, you know – of course I did have the cataracts done. But people just stepped in and, you know, my sister-in-law came up at 7 o'clock in t'morning and took 'em to school, brought 'em back. My friend came, 'Right, Jane, I'll have 'em tomorrow. Bring 'em to my house for tea.' I have got a good circle of friends.

I try to bring 'em up right. Because you see some children, they're right rough. My boys are polite. They both read really well. But you see, I've read with 'em every night. I hear some parents at school saying, 'Well I don't, because it's not my job. Teachers get paid for doing that.' And I'll say, 'But it only takes you 10 minutes.' It's enjoyable, you know: 'Sit here, let's read', and t'telly goes off. No distractions. I'll read a bedtime story for 'em.

I know what a life they would have had, if I hadn't got them. It would have been too late. And now I've got the say, and you know that you're doing the right thing for 'em. It's just being terrified of what might happen in the future. As they get older we sometimes have clashes over things, and it's harder now William has gone on to secondary and they are at separate schools. We have a military operation to get ready in a morning. How I wish I could sometimes have a lie-in! But they are doing well at school and I'm very proud of 'em. William has settled in well at his new school, though recently he has been bullied and I'm trying to deal with that now.

The boys are good friends as well. William still remembers the violence when they were with Ian, and they both seem content to be living with Gran. The Residence Order allowance comes in so useful for bus fares, taxis, school clothes and shoes. And since Harry died I've had such a lot of help from people and have made friends I would never have known. Life can be a challenge but to see them growing up is worth everything. If only Ian was not still letting them down! Sometimes you have your down days and think, 'Why am I doing this? Why?' And then you think, 'But I know why I'm doing it' – because you feel a bond with them and I love 'em so much.

* * *

Editorial Commentary

Many features of this account resonate with Caroline Archer's analysis in the Afterword. We see how very young children were traumatised by alcoholic parents, who neglected them badly and abused them physically and verbally. There is a vivid description of how trauma presents itself – in extreme fearfulness leading to overcompliant behaviour at school, whilst anger and 'acting-out' behaviours are released in the perceived safer setting of home. Neurobiological impairment is also suggested in the hyperactive behaviour of the younger child (who was eventually diagnosed with attention deficit hyperactivity disorder (ADHD) at age 11 and is now being offered help).

Particularly striking in this story is the way grandchildren were 'dumped' on grandparents who were quite unprepared. There was no serious assessment of them or their circumstances, no financial or psychological support and undue pressure to sign forms that were not fully explained to them. Apart from the initial court case, no medical attention to the possible impact of parental alcoholism was forthcoming. It has taken many years for Jane to begin to access the help she and the children needed from the outset.

The impact on family relationships when adult children become addicted and subsequently maltreat their children is incalculable. It is very painful for Jane to admit what her son has done, and bewildering to make sense of how he turned to drink. It is only a slight relief to blame most of the situation on his wife – a judgement that the court confirms. Yet their son remains with his wife and barely visits his children. Despite Jane's heroic efforts, the children remain in danger of being retraumatised, as events and memories trigger sensory and emotional responses.

The fortitude and resilience that many grandparents display and their capacity to redefine their role in the most adverse of circumstances (including death) are well illustrated here. The part that self-help groups can play is also underlined – such groups provide a safe place where grandparents can turn to each other without fear, stigma or misunderstanding. They can support grandparents to find information and seek other friends to break the isolation that caring for young children often brings, alongside allowing their grandchildren to discover that they are not alone.

2

Dorothy

'I'm Mum, Dad and Grandma'

Dorothy's daughter, Louise, had a violent relationship with Eddie, a manipulative substance abuser. They had one child, Izzie, before the marriage collapsed. Louise tried to make a fresh start with another partner, Adam, and had a second child, Joe, but Eddie went on harassing her and she committed suicide. Dorothy took on Izzie after Louise died and for a time also shared the care of Joe with his father.

* * *

When Izzie was around 10–11 months old, and still being bottle-fed, Louise phoned me to say, 'Mum, I'm at the Bradford Royal Infirmary with Izzie, can you come quickly and will you bring clothes, bottles and x, y and z?' I said, 'What on earth's happened?' 'I'll tell you when you get here.' Later Louise told me that after a minor quarrel, Eddie had thrown the baby's bottle at her, and then struck her hard on the side of the head – and she dropped Izzie! And Izzie bounced off the corner of the washing machine, onto the kitchen floor. Then it was something like 2 hours before he would allow her to take Izzie to the hospital. That was the thing he used to do – he used to hold them hostage.

I was just finishing work at school, where I was a teacher. I rushed to the hospital. Louise was with Izzie in this little side assessment room, absolutely tearful, with quite a few people in there. Blood had been streaming down the side of her neck, where he had hit her hard, behind her ear. She was being given first aid and there were quite a few people around Izzie's cot. I said, 'I'm here now. I'll look after Izzie.' Eddie wasn't there. The police arrived and Louise was shown out into another room where she could be interviewed. And, as the paediatrician was checking out Izzie, he was asking me questions – 'You know, I've got an idea roughly about what's gone on, but what on earth do you think caused it? Was he drunk do you think?' I said, 'No, he doesn't drink.' Then he said, 'What about drugs?' Now I didn't know it at the time – I had *not a clue*. It was only later that I learnt he was just taking everything. So I said, 'I don't think so, I don't know that he does drugs.' He said, 'Well, what is it then?' I said, 'Just temper'. 'Oh', he said, 'That's even worse. You haven't an excuse then.'

Anyway, they kept Izzie in overnight but she smiled at me when I went in next day. She was okay. Of course Eddie was arrested but he only got community service or something – just the softly, softly treatment.

Louise was only a tiny little dot, only 17 when she met and married Eddie. And he already looked like he knew what he was after. He was very manipulative. As soon as I saw him, I thought, 'He's not for you Louise.' He was older than her, by about 9 years, physically, but mentally by about 19 years. And my daughter was one of these that the more you forbade her to do something, or you counselled her against something, well, she would do it. So you used to bite your tongue and bide your time. Because I just knew he was trouble. And she ended up being strangled by him, being knocked out by him. She would come in the middle of the night with Izzie and bang on the door – she would have bruises on her neck. She would have strangle marks, she would be in pieces. Louise and Izzie lived here more than they lived at her own house. Sometimes she would send me a text: 'He's being an idiot Mum, can you come round?' He would get very hyperactive and his tone of voice would change and she would know he was just starting. I would go over – he knew I would call the police if he did anything. And I would say, 'I thought we were going shopping Louise? Come on, get your coat on, hurry up, I've got Izzie with me.' And that would defuse the situation.

Social Services were involved on numerous occasions, after the police had been called to caution and warn him. Social Services did come round to Louise and they said, 'If you continue to take this man back, and risk your daughter, we may have to take her away from you.' And I think then, the gravity of the situation, whereby external forces could do things that would be out of her hands – I think that made her see sense. But leaving him was another matter. For Eddie, who probably has borderline personality disorder, having somebody reject you is like a red rag to a bull. And then, he would give her all sorts of reasons as to why *she* was making *him* behave in the way he was. She was struggling to protect Izzie, but of course it's not just physical, it's the emotional damage that's being done. She and Izzie were both very frightened.

Eddie was well-known to the police, a very unsavoury character. He'd beaten up friends, abused teachers, his own mother. He's very challenging, hates authority – a very clever man, but very devious. He would threaten and abuse Louise and then he would be so contrite and he would phone her, and send her massive bunches of flowers, and say he *loved* her, and he was so *sorry* and he would never do this again. And she would feel sorry for him and…then he would threaten to commit suicide. Before he met Louise he had earned good money. They bought their own house nearby. But he was one of these where everything was done off the record, off the books – he didn't pay tax, pension, pay stamps. He always had a wad full of money in his back pocket, but nothing was ever bona fide. And he was dabbling – he would chip computers, PlayStations, £40 a time so that you didn't have to pay for the real game. He would download films to sell. He was put into Armley jail for a short time, when he was selling illegal pirated films and CDs. Meanwhile Louise went into banking and was working her way up. Later she became a seller for a stationery company. It was well rewarded if you got the sales.

After Izzie was hospitalised, Eddie pretty much moved out. He would still come to the house to see Izzie, and he once tried to abduct her from her nursery, even though he wasn't on the list to pick her up. Izzie can even remember Louise saying, 'Hide behind the settee!' cos he was breaking in through the front door. But he kind of kept off the radar until Louise met Adam. I was working, but holidays and weekends, Izzie mostly came and stayed with me. She was a little love. She was at private day nursery during the day, until Louise got home from work and then it was me, and Louise and Izzie.

Louise had by this time, as you can imagine, been put off men. But she'd joined a gym and that was where she met Adam – he was a personal fitness instructor. He was totally different to Eddie. He was very good looking, tall, young, very bright and absolutely besotted – not only with Louise, but with Izzie as well. Izzie was 2 by then. She took to him very quickly, even though, up to then, her idea of men was probably that they shout, they attack Mummy, they do nasty things. And Adam wasn't like that. She still now regards him as Dad – she calls him Daddy. Eventually Louise divorced Eddie and she and Adam had a baby, Joe. They were planning to get married. I've even got the wedding dress in my wardrobe upstairs.

I think it was the Christmas after the divorce, when Izzie was about 4, Eddie came and dropped off her presents at my house – because on Christmas Day I always have all the family with me. And when he came, with this huge box, one of the things I noticed immediately – it was *so* pronounced – was how much weight he had lost. He wouldn't look me in the eye at all. Afterwards we found out that he was a heavy cocaine and crack cocaine user.

When Eddie realised that Louise had got a new partner, he suddenly started demanding rights to see Izzie regularly, which Louise refused. He got himself a solicitor and took her to court. And the court agreed that he should have access to his daughter. But we still didn't know about the drugs. Eddie would have Izzie on a Sunday and he would pick her up from school on a Wednesday, and they would go swimming or do something like that. But it soon became apparent that he was missing contact a lot of the time. Sometimes Louise would be at work, and school would ring to say nobody'd picked Izzie up. And then it would be a case of, 'Mum (that's me!), can you go grab her please, while I make excuses and come out of work?' He started demanding more contact, including overnight stays, which Louise didn't want, because she couldn't trust him.

And Eddie was very jealous. On some occasions, when he had Izzie for contact she'd refer to Adam as her 'dad' – and he took Louise back to court to make the judge tell Louise to make Izzie call *him* 'Daddy' and Adam, 'Adam'.

The judge agreed. But Louise said to me afterwards, 'It doesn't matter what the judge told me. There's no way I'm gonna say that.' It got to the point where Louise just didn't want anything to do with Eddie, and Izzie's behaviour was also becoming difficult – she was having a bit of a bed-wetting problem, and seemed to be anxious. Louise had had Joe by then and Izzie was showing signs of jealousy. And the judge said, 'I think we need to cease contact temporarily, until such time as Eddie can prove that he can commit to this contact and until the mother, Louise, has got some kind of help for Izzie.' But of course that never happened. That must have been round about August 2009 – and then in October 2009, Louise died.

She was only 28 and had been depressed for some time. As well as all the trouble with Eddie, Adam had recently opened a new gym enterprise with my ex-husband, John. It was in its infancy and was very, very hard work. Money was very tight. They had to be very, very driven, and Adam was almost living at the gym 24/7 and Louise almost never saw him. She was kind of having to do everything and I think she got to the point where she just felt it was all too much. It put a huge strain on their relationship, which was already at breaking point. On this particular day, Joe – who at the time was 2 – was in nursery, and Izzie was at the gym with her grandad (John). It was half-term holiday.

Louise had been to work, come home at lunchtime and then spoken to, or saw, everybody who meant something to her. She came and had a cup of tea with me at lunchtime and then said she was off back to work. Then I got a text from her to check that I was collecting Izzie from her grandad's. I replied that I was. When I went to John's he said Louise had been at the gym that afternoon. And I said, 'That's strange because she came and had a cup of tea with me at lunchtime and then she was off back to work – what happened?' He said, 'No, she told us that she was going home – she'd taken the afternoon off to clean, but she came to the gym first.' And I thought, 'That's really odd, that's not like her.' And then John said something that immediately made my heart sink. He said 'Louise said, "The kids would be a lot better off without me."' He brushed it off as just her being a bit silly. But I just knew, I just *knew*. And I said, 'Why didn't you ring me? Why didn't you keep hold of her? Why didn't you...do something?' And he said, 'Why? What's your worry?' I said, 'I've got an awful feeling, John. I just...do...'

I had Izzie with me now, I didn't know what to expect. I drove to where they lived, and the car – she had a people carrier – was parked outside. It was quite dark, so I was surprised there were no lights on. The front door was locked, and we couldn't get in. I hammered, I tried phoning her... But then I remembered the back gate, which wasn't easy to get through. I knew that if I got through there, she very often left her kitchen door round the back unlocked. And we got in and started shouting for her, and then the house phone rang. Izzie picked it up, and it was Adam at the gym. 'Dorothy, where's Louise? I've just had a phone call from the nursery [this was just after 6 o'clock – normally it closes then] and Joe hasn't been picked up. Where is she?' I said, 'Adam, I don't know. I'm at your house. It's all in darkness. I've got in because she hasn't locked the back door but I can't find her.' And he said, 'Oh, maybe she's gone to the nursery to pick him up.' And I said, 'The car's outside. She hasn't gone to the nursery.' And Izzie was shouting, 'Mummy! Mummy! I can't find her!'

I walked into the bedroom and she was laid, face down, in a big pile of clothes. Adam said, 'I'm coming home, now.' And I turned her over, and she was already blue around her lips. Her finger ends were blue. And she was really warm – her fingers were cold, but she was warm. And Izzie screamed, 'Is Mummy dead?' And I said, 'Sweetheart, I don't think so. I think she's just collapsed and I think she's very poorly. Can you go downstairs please – I'm going to call the ambulance now, but because your house is a bit awkward to find, you might have to wave to them and tell them where we are.' I turned her over, and oh, dreadful!... I just cuddled her and cradled her and said, 'I love you – why? What have you done?'

I found an empty packet of pills. It was a powerful antidepressant and sleeping mixture. It was prescribed to her by a GP that was new to our practice – he didn't know her. Dangerously, he'd given her 2 months' supply. I was later informed by the coroner's office that she had no alcohol or other drugs in her system.

On the very day that Louise died, a bailiff came round to serve a warrant on Louise – Eddie wanted to restart contact. We were all here, grieving, in a state of turmoil and shock. And I was outside in the garden, just ranting at the world. And the bailiff said, 'I've got a court warrant, Louise needs to be back in court.' And I just looked at him and I said, 'She's dead. She died.'

When the bailiff took the news of Louise's death back to Eddie's solicitor, I got her phoning me on my mobile, asking, 'Was there any foul play?' I put the phone down on her. Then Eddie kept ringing my phone and eventually it was my younger daughter Laura that answered it. I won't repeat her language. It was quite colourful and used a lot of expletives, but more or less she said, 'I blame you for a lot of this, what you put her through.'

So I actually took Izzie and Joe the night that we found her mum dead. Adam was in a world of his own, but later he took Joe to stay with him. Joe turned 3 a month after she died. Can you imagine? Louise had even arranged his birthday party! All that had been booked and paid for. He had his birthday party and seemed to recover, but Izzie struggled. And what followed was that I then had to fight Eddie in court to get Izzie, after Louise had fought him for 5 years over access to Izzie. One of the solicitors said to me that this was one of the longest private family cases that they'd ever been involved with in Yorkshire. It ended with me being awarded a Special Guardianship for Izzie, 3 years after Louise's death.

After Louise died I immediately went to her solicitor, who already knew everything...had represented her in court. What I didn't know was that she was a senior law partner and, as such, her fees were, at the time (this is going back 5 years) something like £185 an hour. By the end of the first year, I had already eaten through £14,000 of my retirement pension – and there was no end in sight. She said, 'This is going to be an ongoing battle.' She warned me it was going to be very, very costly. I wasn't entitled to any kind of financial help. And neither was Louise. And yet Eddie was. He got everything paid for through legal aid. Louise did at one point have financial aid, but when Adam moved in with her, there were two wages – she was honest about it, and they cut her financial help. She tried to represent herself in court and sometimes she would get very angry and shout out and then be sent out. I attended court on many occasions with Louise, as her buddy, her friend – you know, the 'McKenzie friend'. You're not allowed to speak, but you are allowed to support the person. At one point the court actually asked me if I wouldn't mind supervising the contact with Izzie because sometimes those two were just getting into an argument. I didn't want to be the supervisor, but they didn't feel it was going to be good for Izzie to involve a third party. But later, Eddie's solicitor told me that this was a private court case, and Louise shouldn't be discussing anything with me and it was not my right to know. I had to keep completely out of it. Luckily the judge disagreed and told her off publicly.

When I realised how costly the ongoing case would be, I saw that, like Louise, I would have to represent myself. It's actually not very nice, because they're talking *about* you, but they're talking *to* you, because you are on both sides. But I got hold of all Eddie's medical notes and discovered the extent of his problems and addictions. At the very first hearing I was awarded a Residence Order for Izzie, and the court appointed a guardian ad litem.[1] But Eddie was still wanting to restart contact, straight after her mum had died, after I hadn't seen him for months and months. He said he knew his daughter best. I just said definitely not. After what that little girl's been through, and what this family, just starting their grief, has been through! But Eddie was allowed contact, though it was reduced, and a lot of the time Izzie would scream and cry because she didn't even want to go with him. I didn't make her go, but then he would curse and say I'd poisoned her mind.

Eventually I decided to go for a Special Guardianship. Eddie would have preferred it if I'd just had a Residence Order, where I was supposed to involve him in big decisions like which school she went to, medication and so on. With a Special Guardianship you are supposed to keep parents informed, but you don't actually have to consult with them. Eddie was still fighting for face-to-face contact. The big final contested court case took place 3 years ago and I was awarded the Special Guardianship. By the end of the second day the female judge had already made up her mind that I was going to get it, after Eddie lost his rag in the witness box. It came up in court that Eddie has a history of attacking partners – in at least one case the police were involved after he beat a girlfriend. Eddie would argue against anyone in authority. In court he tried to say the police had got it all wrong.

An independent psychologist said that he was in complete denial of his wrong-doings with Louise – he could not see the big part he has played and he could not put Izzie's needs before his own. He didn't act as the adult and she couldn't recommend that he have access to Izzie unsupervised. In the end Eddie was told he could not reapply to the court for any reconsideration of contact unless he had undergone significant therapy that had been assessed to have made a difference.

Getting Help for Izzie

At the same time that all this was going on, I was trying to get help for Izzie. She had her seventh birthday, in the January, after Mummy died in the previous October. Adam arranged her party – she had a swimming party. Lots of people came – that was lovely, a success. At primary school they were already very much in the loop, they knew all about it and they put lots of things into place for her. But Izzie wouldn't go to sleep without me. She wouldn't go to bed without me. She woke up through the night and got in bed with me. Eventually it got to the point that so long as I was upstairs, banging the drawers and the cupboards in my room, so she could hear that I was upstairs, that was okay. But if she wasn't quite asleep when I came down, she would come down – she would come downstairs anything up to 9, or 10, 11 times. And I would take her back up and stay with her, sometimes until the wee small hours, and neither of us had any sleep.

I can remember once just saying, 'Izzie, tell me what it is. Just tell me, because I am trying to help here, but I need to know what it is.' 'Because', I said, 'it's not the stairs, it's not the dark, cos you've lived here since you've been a baby – and you used to sleep absolutely fine.' I said, 'You have to tell me.' She says, 'I can't, Nana, cos you'll laugh at me.' I said, 'Look at my face – do I look like I'm going to laugh at you? Because I'm not.' So she said, 'If I fall asleep, what if something happens to you whilst I'm asleep and I don't know what to do then and I'm left all on my own?' So I said, 'OK, that's a good question. All right, we'll do something about it.'

I bought her a very easy, child-friendly, little address book, and I put all the key people that she could contact – she knew how to use the phone and she could read, almost independently, by the time she was 4. And I said, 'Nothing is going to happen to me – but should you feel that you need to contact somebody, these are the phone numbers of everybody you know and you can contact.' I also set up a worry box for her. I got the idea from a fabulous book that I used to read at school in assembly, called *The Huge Bag of Worries*.[2] Once you unzip the bag and all the worries come out and you can see them, a lot of them disappear. A lot of them you can do something with right now. A lot of them you have to think about and put aside. We had bits of paper and pencils, and when she had a worry she would write it on this piece of paper and post it into the worry box and then at a nice, calm and quiet time, we'd open up the worry box together and pull out all the bits of paper, and I'd say, 'Right – that's nothing for you to worry about, I can deal with that', and so on. This worry box lasted for about a couple of months. And then, after that, she thought that she could just talk to me about it.

My health visitor helped me to get bereavement counselling for Izzie through the Family Loss Project when she was just turned 7. I think a lot of Izzie's tantrums, then and now, have all been about control – she couldn't control her mum's death and she's afraid it will happen again. The counsellor from the Family Loss Project came, and explained that the thing about bereavement counselling is that it can be extremely useful, very therapeutic, but you have to get the timing right. If the timing isn't right, it's not beneficial at all. I asked, 'Can you assess Izzie, to see if she's ready?' They decided to try. A lot of it was play therapy – modelling clay, painting, glueing and sticking. I know *now* that there are a lot of things that Izzie couldn't discuss with me about her mum, because she thought it would upset me. She didn't want to upset me so she kept that bottled up. But I thought if she could talk to somebody that was non-judgemental and who wasn't going to break down, they might get Izzie to open up. But do you know what? Izzie never did. She never opened up to anybody. And then we went through a period when she was about 9, 10, of her becoming quite disruptive at home, quite challenging and abusive, and I referred her back to the Family Loss Project.

Round about this time I decided to take early retirement from my teaching job, where I had a lot of responsibilities. There was just no way, with all this going on – and I was still fighting in court as well – my heart wasn't in it. And it suddenly makes you realise what's important in life. I mean I would even lock up with the caretaker at half past six, and still have my homework to sort out and planning to do. I'd already had a lot of time out on the grounds of bereavement, and the school were very good with that. And then the head that I had worked so well with for so many years had taken early retirement, and the new head that we'd got in her place, just – I didn't gel with her. Eventually I said, 'I can't give the commitment that I did before. I just think it's time for me to call it a day.'

Not long after this though, there was another tragedy. My younger daughter, Laura, became disabled after a brain stem stroke. She was in intensive care with pneumonia – double pneumonia – and she had the stroke at the end of the first week. We were told more or less she wouldn't survive, but miraculously she pulled through. This was only 2 years after Louise died. When she was in intensive care, I almost lived in the hospital. Thank goodness for Adam, he had Izzie and Joe. I had one of these put-you-up beds next to Laura in intensive care. In hospital they were *really* good, they were absolutely marvellous. But she's been let down since. She should have had a lot of physiotherapy and rehabilitation, and there was just not enough money. She can't stand, she's got quite a weak right side, her speech is very slurred – but her mind is all there. Her short-term memory is terrible; her long-term memory is really good. She's married and she's got two boys – one who is nearly the same age as Izzie. Both my girls were pregnant at the same time. There are not many siblings who are best friends like they were. She lives nearby and her husband is marvellous – he's a rock. But sometimes I have to go and help to look after her.

Had things been as they should be, even with Louise's death, then, if something happened to me, Izzie would have gone to live with Laura's family. But with her having a disability now, and with her husband being the main carer, it would be incredibly difficult – even though Izzie's not a young child now, she's older – but they still have two other children. If you ask Auntie Laura how many kids have you got, she will sometimes say, 'I've got three.' She includes Izzie. But I don't know that they would have a very strong case to allow Izzie to live there, considering that Laura is very, very poorly.

So Izzie had suffered another loss – her auntie – and she became angry and harder to manage. She was violent, she used to throw things, kick. I gave her really good suggestions: 'When you feel your temper rising, these are the kind of things you can do – tear up paper, punch a pillow, go and listen to some music. You know, open your windows, shout

out loud, that kind of thing. Leave Nana alone, walk away.' But she can't – she used to follow me around the house. So if *I* tried to walk away she would follow me. She *wanted* confrontation.

I went back to the Family Loss Project. I said, 'I'm wondering whether this anger is because she is ready now for bereavement counselling – maybe she is ready now to rant and rave at the world and "Why haven't I got a mum?" Maybe this is her time. And she's taking it out on me, because I'm the nearest one. Is she pushing me away? Is she thinking, "I'll walk away"? Her dad's walked away, her mum's left her. She's abandoned... And she's testing me – how easily will I go as well? Will I abandon her?' The project took her in fairly quickly for more bereavement counselling. But again she did not open up. They went as far as they could and eventually I was told that if there were still issues with Izzie, then I needed a referral to CAMHS [Child and Adolescent Mental Health Services].

Meanwhile our relationship got worse – she would completely refuse to go to bed and I was getting no sleep at all. And then tempers are fraught. And you really get to the point where you think, 'What am I doing wrong? You know – this isn't good, not just for me, it's not good for her. And why is it happening like this? I'm doing everything I can. Can she not see that?' But she's a child – 'course she can't see that. I'm the only one there for her, but you take it out on your nearest and dearest, don't you? And it got to the point where I was ringing Social Services at about 11 o'clock at night, speaking to the duty social workers. One of them said, 'Look Dorothy, you know Izzie, better than anybody. What do you think might help?' And I said, 'If I can defuse the situation, by making light of it, before it gets to the really angry part – if you can crack a joke at yourself or poke fun at yourself – that can work.' One night I was talking to the duty social worker and Izzie was having a tantrum, and I'm trying to walk away from her. She was waving her arms and legs around, and I just happened to say, 'Oh good grief! I've got an octopus on the floor now!' And that was it. I didn't mean it as a joke! You know – I was just trying to say, 'all arms and legs' – and immediately, Izzie just saw the lighter side to it and I said to the worker, 'That's it, I think we're going to be okay.' And Izzie immediately came and gave me a cuddle... and we gave each other a cuddle, and I said, 'Right, now it's bedtime.' And I went up with her and gave her a big hug and said, 'Nana's going to be here for you Izzie, no matter what you do.' I said, 'I don't always like you, but I will always love you. But it would be quite nice if we could try and get on with each other.'

I got a referral to CAMHS after Izzie put a comment on Facebook: 'I wish I was dead.' Alarm bells started ringing and I went to the GP, but it was the school nurses who came to talk about all the emotional problems that Izzie had had. They put in an urgent referral to CAMHS, that same day. I had a phone call by the Wednesday and I had a meeting with CAMHS by the Friday. This was a couple of years ago. We went to CAMHS for a long time, and they prescribed melatonin to help her to sleep, but most of it was talking therapy and a lot of the time Izzie just wasn't engaged with it. They said that it's a two-way process, and if the young person or adolescent doesn't want to engage, there's no magic wand. If they want to be there, they can work with them. If they don't want to be there, they either have to wait until they're ready, or they just chip away and chip away, with the same message.

Meanwhile Izzie suffered another blow. Adam had been deeply affected by Louise's death. For many years he couldn't face life. He was running away. He would go abroad for months at a time. He was doing the most dreadful sorts of security services, in the parts of Africa, and India and even

Afghanistan, that even our own soldiers won't go, because it's so dangerous. And then I had both Izzie and Joe. Joe was almost like, shared. When Adam did come back, then Joe would go and stay with his daddy. But because we were so close at the time, he stayed here quite a lot as well. Then there was a period when Adam stayed in Bradford. It was quite a nice arrangement because we always said we'd try and keep the kids together, whenever we could. We both got on with our lives, but if I was going out somewhere, I'd take them both and give him some time off or he would take them somewhere. He would take them to school, and give me some time.

But then he met this other girl who had her own son, and they moved out with Joe. Joe was staying with Dad and now had this other little boy to play with, and Izzie perhaps felt a little bit left out, but she wouldn't stay at Adam's. And in the end the new partner said, 'Let's move away from Bradford. Let's have a complete clean break.' Adam knew that it would break my heart that he was taking Joe, and he didn't know how to break it to me. I knew Izzie wouldn't go, because she wanted to be here with me.

They went to live in Wales. Izzie visits now and again, and Joe visits us, but it took us a while before Adam and I got back together again and for me to trust him. Adam and his new partner have just recently had a new baby together. It broke Izzie's heart when Joe went. She's lost her auntie, she's lost her mum, she hasn't had a real dad. Her step-dad that she calls 'Dad' has moved away, and has now got his own nice little family, because they've taken Joe. When Joe came up this half-term, the night before he was due to go back to Wales, Izzie said, 'I don't want Joe to go back, Nana.' I think she really misses having a little brother here. They fight like cat and dog obviously at times, but the rest of the time – you know we did so much together – they went swimming, to a play centre, we did parks, we did the Media Museum, visited friends.

Eddie Reappears

Adam and his partner have had their ups and downs. One day they had a fight and the police were called and Social Services were involved. The incident was settled and it was deemed there was no risk to the children, but it made the local newspaper and somehow Eddie found this and realised that Izzie still occasionally spent time with Adam. He rang Social Services and said, 'I don't want my daughter going to Adam's – I think he's a bully.'

Two years after I got the Special Guardianship, Eddie reappeared, claiming he has had extensive therapy. And he had also been contacting Izzie through Twitter and messaging her on Facebook. We have kept copies. The other thing he's done – Izzie's at secondary school now and her school phoned me to say, 'Do you know that there's a gentleman called Eddie phoning all the schools in the area to find out which school Izzie goes to?' Unfortunately he is allowed to know this, but he is not allowed to access her. But she's 12 now and she's got to make up her own mind. I've explained to her that he's been battling with a lot of addictions, he's got mental health issues and he is too much of a needy character. He needs to see to himself before he can put her needs first. But she is still curious, especially now that Adam is no longer around to be seen as her dad. At her new school she hasn't told anybody she hasn't got a mum, because people treat you as different. On Facebook they play silly games like 'Five things that worry you the most', and she wrote, 'Number one – we just had a big row and Nana might kick me out. Number two – spiders, and number three – my real dad might find me...' Her grandad (my ex-husband) saw this and responded. He told her, 'Number one wouldn't happen because your Nana wouldn't allow it and she'd never let you go. Number three wouldn't happen cos *I* wouldn't let it happen.'

At one time Izzie became extremely violent, to the point where I had to phone the police, and she was arrested and put in police cells for about 5 hours. I ended up with bruises all over. Then the Youth Offending Team were involved, and a placement support officer. I said, 'We are going to end up killing one another. I feel like I'm being abused and threatened in my own home. I feel...powerless because she is a child and I can't just turn round and do something back to her.' And I said, 'You know, it's really getting to a point where I don't know what to do for the best. Should I say, "That's it. Enough. Somebody else take her just for a little while?"' But the placement support officer said, 'Dorothy, you *are* the best person for her. You've gone through it together. *You* know this little girl better than anybody.' And they did some therapy work with us – sometimes separate, sometimes together, around identity, values, family life, what makes a family.

But they also put me in touch with something called Acres – Adolescent, Crisis, Respite. They come in to give respite to the young person and the carers, the parents. It's only short term, but they did do quite a lot of work with her. One thing they talked about was scenarios – this child has done this to the parents and what kind of help do they need? They said that Izzie would come up absolutely spot on – I think this is what the child should do, I think these are the rules, they should get help, this is what the parents should do, there should be a bit of compromise, they should listen to one another. But then, they changed the scenario – she's a girl who has unfortunately lost her mum and lives with her grandma and is not terribly nice at times. She knew immediately that was her. She wasn't going to play that game. The hood went up, she closed herself up and she moved to the other end of the settee. With Izzie, there could be an awful lot locked inside.

The thought of Eddie resurfacing makes me feel very anxious, and I have been advised that I might have to seek the help of a solicitor again, to find out what my rights are. For a start-off he isn't supposed to be contacting her in any way, shape or form, other than via letterbox – that is in the Court Order. But of course court is long since finished. I've contacted the police and they said, 'Has he made any threats?' I said, 'No, not at all.' So they said, 'Well to be honest, we can't do anything unless he is actually intimidating; if he comes to your door, if he hangs around the school, then we can take action.' I've contacted the school as well and they are very aware that if anybody called Eddie comes, he's not allowed. What we can't stop him from doing, unfortunately, is if he wanted to buy, say, tickets to the Christmas carol concert, he could go and watch her. And if she comes out of the school grounds – and he's there...

The judge had written into the final Court Order that there shall be letterbox contact by way of an exchange of cards, postcards, gifts, letters – there is an expectation for birthdays, Christmas day, Father's day and so on. In the early days his cards and letters were checked over by the guardian or Social Services, and one or two of them were deemed unsuitable. The birthday before last he must have left it too late to post a card and he came to the house and posted it! She was in bed. Then one day, a couple of years ago, he'd written something like 'Hi' to her on Facebook, and she'd put, 'Hi back, who's this?' And he said, 'Eddie'. And she'd put something like, 'You're not supposed to contact me, only just letterbox contact.' And he'd put, 'I do write letters. I don't think your Nana gives you them all (which I do). Don't get cross at me, everything you may have been told will not be the truth.' You know, in other words, he will still try and convince himself and Izzie that it is me and Adam keeping him away from her.

This birthday just gone was different. Normally he plays safe, and sends a card with money in it. 'To a wonderful daughter', 'I love you and miss you, kiss, kiss, kiss' – that kind of thing. But this time he sent books, chocolates, a bath bubbly set and a big long letter. Now this letter, I think the latest girlfriend's helped him to write it: 'Do you remember when we used to go swimming together?' It's like he's trying to bring back, relive, the things that they used to do. But Izzie looked at it and she said, 'Anybody could have written that letter and he might just have signed it! Anybody could have written that, Nana.'

Eddie is trying to twist Izzie's mind by saying, 'I don't think Nana gives you all my letters.' It makes me really cross that he doesn't acknowledge all I do. I can remember once, in one of the court hearings, when Eddie was there, one of the solicitors actually said, 'Do you know what? At the top of all this, through all this grief, through all of this that Dorothy has been through, where she has put her life on hold – her retirement has been sacrificed, to bring up this little girl – and she's doing a damned good job and nobody's saying, "Thank you for that."' I'm not looking for any kind of, you know, accolade, but at least it was recognised. I'm not going to get that from Eddie. I also got a text once from the long-term social worker. It came out of the blue and she just said, 'Dorothy, you're doing an absolutely marvellous job. Just keep going. Don't worry about Eddie: just keep doing what you're doing. Because I don't think anybody else would have the commitment, you know, juggling everything.' And at Acres, one of the workers said, 'Oh aren't you fabulous!' And I said, 'I don't feel fabulous, I'm just not getting a handle on her. Why can't I? I could make other kids – I could, you know, make kids at school do – why can't I make my own granddaughter do?'

For Izzie though, I'm Mum, Dad *and* Grandma. The other day she said to me, 'Nana, am I an only child?' And I said, 'It must feel like it sweetheart, it must do. But you're not really.' Not only does she have Joe – I know he's her half-brother, but he's the nearest thing to a full-blood brother – but both Eddie and Adam have grown-up children by other partners. But in practice she's only got me – that's it. And Izzie and I have lost that normal grandma relationship that I still have with Joe. I'm no longer taking him to school every day, washing his clothes every day, cutting his toenails – you know, I just have him for holidays and weekends. That dreadful summer that they moved to Wales – we went as a family to Northumberland, including Joe, the dog and John. John and I get on really quite well. It was lovely. But then we came back and it was just – Izzie and I.

We do have some good times though. The best times are when we are cuddling, when she's actually agreeing to do the right things. At the moment I'm not getting so much of the poorer times. We do fight more than anything over use of the internet, but you know, we have rules, she doesn't have the phone on at night. She does take the phone to bed because she reads on it – Kindle-type things. But I can actually disable the Wi-Fi and she never has any credit on her phone. Having Joe here this week has been lovely, because she's done the kind of things that children should be doing. I've taken all four grandchildren together and we've met with family, and we've had ice creams, they've run around being silly, she's been a little girl – and it's been lovely to see her like that. We've gone swimming, she's looked after her little brother, they've read stories – it's all that kind of thing – it's her coming up and putting her arms round me and saying, 'I love you Nana.'

Having the Special Guardianship has made a difference. Izzie got into our first choice of secondary schools. If she'd been in care for even one night I would have got more help, but I couldn't have put my granddaughter into care! It's *unthinkable*.

I don't know what would happen to her if I get ill or worse. I've thought about this long and hard. I know that Social Services look at placing children with friends and family first, but with Laura's illness that would now be very difficult. Other than that, Izzie herself would have a voice, because I think by the age of 12, if they are quite intelligent and mature in their thoughts, then they [Social Services] will take into consideration the child's views. I think, if anything, it would be Adam, because she's saying to me now, 'It must be nice to have a family again, like Joe has.' She doesn't know their ups and downs, and I would like to think that for Joe's sake Adam and his partner are going to stick together and have stability.

Sharing with Other Grandparents

In all this uncertainty The Grandparents Group has helped enormously. I first heard about it from the school nurse. She said, 'I want you to consider going.' But when she said it was at the Bridge Project, it kind of rang warning bells, because the only person I had known who had anything to do with the Bridge Project had been Eddie. But she said, 'I think it would be beneficial for you to meet other grandparents – you need an outlet; you need not to be on your own.' So I met with Mary a few times and I remember the first time I told her my story – she was in tears and we were both sharing tissues. Then I got to see all these grandparents busy chatting and knowing each other, and I thought, 'How lovely'.

The first time I ever went to The Grandparents Group, it was actually what you might call 'full house', and I was just bowled over by the amount of people in the same boat as me. You think you're isolated. And you think, 'There's only me' and 'Am I doing things the right way?' and 'What would others make of that?' and 'Why can't I just be a grandparent and give them back again?' Social life – I've lost all of that. But to hear other people's stories made me feel I fit in quite nicely here, I'm not the odd one out – there's lots of us. And we're doing a damned good job, between us, we really are. I just don't think there's enough made of us, or enough help.

* * *

Editorial Commentary

In this case, Dorothy's adult daughter became the victim of a long-term substance user and ended up taking her own life. When the grandmother stepped in to take on her young granddaughter, she found she has no right to protection from legal harassment by the child's father. This highlights the serious issue of perpetrators being *enabled* to threaten the provision of a safe environment for a traumatised child. This occurred despite the man having a criminal record, his violent behaviour being known to the authorities and considerable doubt about his fitness to be in contact with his child having been voiced at previous legal proceedings. The issue of confidentiality is also raised. A person with parental rights (in this case a Special Guardianship Order) does not have access to important information relevant to the situation – namely the father's history of drug abuse, only disclosed when she took on her own case in court.

The chaotic fall-out from substance abuse affects families at all levels of society. Although this grandparent had a professional job and considerable knowledge and personal resources, and several agencies were involved, the help to make a difference has not yet materialised. Furthermore, because she had savings, she lost out through having to fund the legal process to protect the child.

Like others in our accounts, this child has seen domestic violence, and suffered immeasurably from losing her mother. She was clearly traumatised, convinced that further loss and abandonment will be her lot, and she resisted being comforted.

Instead she became challenging and violent herself and strove to drag her grandmother into the chaos. What matters to children like this is that their grandparents do not abandon or give up on them. This grandmother has managed to stand firm, although at great cost to herself (job loss, pension seriously diminished, even her own safety). School nurses figure again in this story, in drawing her attention to The Grandparents Group, where at least she is able to share her story amongst others who face the same dilemmas and crises.

Notes

1. This is an independent officer appointed by a family court to ensure that children's interests are fully addressed and served. This task is now handled through a body called Cafcass (Children and Family Court Advisory and Support Service).

2. Ironside, V. (1996) *The Huge Bag of Worries*. London: Hodder Wayland.

3

Kathleen

She said, 'I don't have a problem'

Kathleen, 61, is caring for her two grandchildren, Kelly and Katy. Their mother, Lara, is Kathleen's youngest daughter – a heroin addict who is now seriously ill. Kathleen's son, Ben, died in his early 20s of a drug overdose.

* * *

Kelly was born when my daughter Lara were 19. She'd been on drugs from 15 and then she met Kelly's father, who'd just been released from prison. When Kelly were born they were both on heroin. She told me she'd stopped using and I believed her. I warned the pair of them, the day that child were born – the first sign of drugs, the Social Services were going to be involved. No second chances. They said, 'We're not silly, we know that.' But because Lara were using drugs during the pregnancy, Kelly were in the special care unit. The day that Kelly were born, her father, Steve, robbed the payphone in the baby intensive care unit, and blamed another father, though I didn't know this at the time. This was the kind of man he was. They kept Kelly in hospital 10 days as a precaution – because of the heroin, but also because Lara were on breathing tablets. She'd been seriously asthmatic since she were 6. The medication stayed in her system 24 hours, so they had to make sure that Kelly were breathing of her own accord and not because these tablets had got into her system. Anyway, Kelly were fine – she didn't show much sign of drug abuse.

They brought her home from hospital when she were 10 days old. And on the way home from hospital they called here – and left her wi'me! For the weekend – this wan't prearranged! At that time I'd only got a small pack o'nappies in – I had to go out and buy nappies and formula. But I thought, 'Right, Lara can get a good night's sleep.' Lara was very immature – she was 19, but to look at her, you'd think she were 14. And to be honest, I thought, maybe she was incapable of looking after a baby. Steve was older than her. He would have been probably 23, 24. Anyway they came back on Sunday, for their dinner, and then took Kelly home, cos I were working Monday morning. And this went on from then.

An Earlier Tragedy

The nightmare of drugs had started with Ben, my son. He got onto drugs when he were about 15, 16. I were totally clueless at the time. I'd no contacts with drugs whatsoever. One day his friend let out what was happening and you could have knocked me down with a feather! I hadn't a clue and me head were all over the place. I knew he'd been going to the doctor's so I rung and said, 'Look, I've just found out my son's on drugs. Can you tell me what's going on?' And he said, 'I'm sorry I can't.' Confidentiality.

When Ben got on to it, it were all the raves [impromptu parties organised through social media]. And his so-called friends had given him heroin, but he didn't know it were heroin until after. They didn't tell him. And the first time he injected, his friends held him down and injected him. By the time I eventually found out, I didn't know another soul whose kids were on drugs. You know, I were just out of my league. I were mortified, I felt so embarrassed, yeah, it was shame! I didn't tell any of me family, me father or me sisters or anybody. Nobody knew, except me, Lara and me eldest daughter, Leanne. And by then kids were shouting at Leanne and Lara – 'Your brother's a smackhead!' So Lara had seen that side of it, before she got mixed up in it. Leanne were spending as much time as she could *away* from the house, because she just couldn't stand it. Leanne and Ben were always close. But Ben were such a *nice* lad. He were a *lovely* lad.

Eventually I had police searching the house for stuff, though they didn't find anything. Ben were arrested over and over again for stealing – he always got caught! On his first time in court I actually asked the solicitor to come down hard. I said, 'Give him, you know, probation – anything, to give him the short, sharp shock.' They wouldn't do it. And he did steal from me – not a lot, but I used to have to hide me purse, because the money'd disappear. And I didn't have a lot of money! I were a single parent with three children. Since Lara were little, I've always done it on me own. I had a good job, in a solicitor's office.

But then, for about 6 years Ben was *trying* to sort himself out. He started to go to a centre where they took in and helped drug addicts. And then he met this girl – she were lovely – no drugs, no nothing. And he'd got himself onto the blockers that they did then, to stop you tekking – if you took heroin you'd be physically sick. He were doing really,

really well. But then he thought he didn't need the centre any more. One day he was at home and I were at work. I'd gone into his bedroom that morning and said, 'I'm really busy today, Ben, please don't come in at work, asking for money.' He said, 'I won't. I promise. I'm sorting meself out now, I'm fine.'

Leanne came home from work to get ready to go out, went into his bedroom – and he was dead on the bed. She rung me up at work, just hysterical. I couldn't mek any sense out of her. All I could hear was, 'He's dead! He's dead! Cold!' And I said, 'Right, I'm coming, I'm coming.' And by the time I got here, there were two ambulances and police and the whole road were blocked off. There were always a mystery about how Ben got the drugs that day, and I had my suspicions that Lara's boyfriend, Steve, brought them to the house, but there was no evidence.

Kelly were 11 months old when Ben died in the August. Lara knew what we'd gone through with Ben, but we didn't even have time to get over *him*, before she were into it. So it's just been like – one thing after another. At the time, I didn't think…well, I believed Lara – or I wanted to believe Lara – that them two, because Kelly were a baby, that they were clean. She wan't. And then, with Ben's death and everything, I took me eye off the ball a bit.

Living with Drugs

Lara were with Steve about 4 years, and then he were caught by the police and imprisoned for several years. Those 4 years were a nightmare. They were both on drugs. They never had any money so I were practically providing everything for Kelly, from the minute she were born. Steve'd never done a day's work in his life, and neither had Lara. I'd got a house for them in Moor End, through a client at work – fully furnished, knives and forks in the drawer, plates and cups in the cupboards. It had, literally, everything. And at first the baby seemed all right. To be fair to Steve, he seemed to do the majority of the caring for her. Lara were in and out of hospital with her asthma and when she'd go into hospital I'd have the baby. And they'd bring her up to me on a weekend and I'd call in from work, just to check on her, on an evening. I thought things wan't too bad – nothing to, sort of, ring alarm bells. But then, around the time of Ben's death, things changed. The furniture in the house started disappearing and Lara claimed a large shed had been stolen from the garden – a big wooden shed! Well *that* rang an alarm bell! I thought, 'No way, that.' And when they were coming and going in the house, there were some gold bracelets of mine that went missing and they insisted, 'It's not us, it's Ben.' Ben said, 'Look Mum, I wouldn't do it, and if I had done it, I'd have owned up to it.' He said, 'But you're not watching Lara.' I said, 'Lara's all right.' He said, 'No she's not.' He ended up dying, taking the blame for those bracelets. And it came out afterwards, it wasn't Ben. It was Steve!

Soon after Ben died, Lara said, 'Can we move out of here [Moor End]?' So I said, 'Why?' She says, 'Cos all Ben's friends keep coming to the door.' By this time I were getting suspicious. I'd twigged on to the fact that these two was back on the drugs. And when I were going down there on an evening – and they were never sure what time I were gonna turn up, I saw there were people coming and going. Some would go as soon as they saw me. They were well-known local addicts whom I knew by then, from me son. So Lara kept saying, 'We want to get away. We don't want to get drawn back into it.' Blah, blah, blah.

I'd put in a landline phone because she were asthmatic, and she needed access to the hospital or an ambulance, and

I was paying the bills – they were sky high. I paid out for Rentokil to come and deal with mice, which they said they had. I don't know whether they came or not. The door got smashed and I ended up having to replace that…

One day when I had Kelly because Lara were in hospital in intensive care, Steve went out stealing for drug money. He climbed in his own mother's window whilst she was at work and stole all these expensive ornaments. Within a couple o' days, he broke into the doctor's unit in the hospital – they caught him on camera, going into the hospital, and they suspected him of taking their wallets and stuff, from their jackets. By this time the police were looking for him and coming to me, because they knew that I were Lara's mother – 'Do you know where he is?' But the police couldn't prove anything.

So anyway, they moved out of Moor End. I were at home then with my older daughter, Leanne, who were at college. Neither of us trusted Steve and I said I wouldn't have him living here. So Lara says, 'Well, if you won't have him here, then we're going into a hostel with Kelly.' I couldn't let Kelly go into a hostel! So then I made the wrong decision, because I let them come. They were here less than a week. Leanne had put a lock on her bedroom door so that they didn't go up in her room. I was at work and Leanne was at college, and Steve took the lock off and stole a necklace which her boyfriend had bought her for Christmas. She accused Steve and I rang the police from work. I thought they were going to kill each other! The police escorted him off the premises.

I said to Lara then, 'Right, I don't want him through that door, ever again.' I said, '*You* can stop, with Kelly, but not him.' 'No, I'm going', said Lara. I said, 'Right, you go with him, but leave the baby here.' 'No. No.' Immediately they got stuff for her and him, took Kelly, didn't even take her bottle or nappies, or a change of clothes. Not a single thing. We were absolutely distraught. This were like 7 o'clock at night. I hadn't a clue where they'd gone.

Of course I rang the police and they said, 'There's nothing we can do, because they're the parents. You've no rights over the child. And, we don't know where they are. Obviously, we'll keep a look out and if we do see them, we'll get in touch with Social Services.' Well, it turned out that they'd gone to Steve's sister who lives in Bosley. He had three sisters living there. One day one of his sisters got in touch wi' me, and she said, 'Look I really need to speak to you. Have you any idea what them two are up to?' I said, 'I don't even know where they are.' She said, 'They're here and there's robberies going on over here!' Lara were on lookout, with the baby, because you wouldn't suspect a young girl with a baby in a pram. They'd done a policeman's house, who was off duty in bed. Steve had gone in, and the policeman chased him. He didn't catch him, but he saw him. And Steve's sister said, 'You know, Lara's back on the drugs.' 'That child', she says, 'She's leaving her in the same nappy all day long, it's literally dripping, sodden! She's got sores on her bottom.' She were around 14 months old. So it all came out. His sister said that Lara and Steve were just literally going round the sisters, dropping Kelly off, disappearing. And the sisters were saying, 'We're all just feeding and looking after this baby.'

So Lara started coming backwards and forwards again here with Kelly, but she'd only come in to drop Kelly off. We didn't know when Lara were going to turn up; *if* she were going to turn up. If I had Kelly at the weekends I knew then she were being dressed and washed and had clean clothes on. We just wanted to make sure that the baby was okay. We took photographs of her bottom and then I rang the doctor who says, 'Take her up to the hospital.' Halfway through the phone call, Lara walked in, realised what were going on, and she just took Kelly! I rung the police and they said, 'She's the mother. We can't do anything.' So I'm getting no back-up whatsoever.

One weekend we hadn't seen or heard of her. I'd rung the hospital, she wan't admitted in there. So I got the bus, up Bosley. I didn't know where I were going. I just wandered round, looking. By this time Lara and Steve had managed to get a house and the sister had given me the address. I asked a bloke if he knew the address and he said, 'Who is it you're looking for? Oh I know them. The door got kicked in yesterday and the windows got smashed.' I said, 'Who by?' He said, 'Drug dealers.' And Steve'd stolen the boiler from this house, three times. Because there was a young child, the council had to replace the boiler, every time. And they had obviously sold them for drugs. I found the house but Lara wouldn't come back home. I hung round till 11 o'clock and came home. We got nowhere.

In the end I contacted Social Services. And I told them what was happening. I said, 'This child is at risk.' They said, 'Well, we've had no reports. Until something happens, we can't do anything.' So I kept ringing up – every week there was something. The police started coming back again, looking for Steve. There were that many warrants out for him and he were on the run. Once Lara rung up and said he'd locked her in the house – 'I can't pick Kelly up because I'm locked in the house, and I can't get out. He's taken all me money.' This is 8 o'clock Sunday night and I'm working, 9 o'clock tomorrow morning. Somehow she got out and met me in town on Monday morning to get the baby, and she were struggling to breathe – which wan't helped, of course, by the drugs and the smoking. I'm back on the phone again to Social Services, but they were still not getting involved.

Then Lara came and she said, 'He's beaten me up. Can I come back home?' So I says, 'Right, you can.' I thought, at least then I'd know what was going on. I said, 'But on condition that Steve comes nowhere near my house.' So she said, 'Right.' And it turns out afterwards, I'm going to work, he's hiding round the corner! As soon as I'd gone on the bus, she were letting him in! But eventually he were arrested and kept on remand. They didn't release him again. It all came out and he ended up serving 6½ years.

Lara Back Home

So then Lara was back home. I was thinking at least now she can sort herself out, without Steve. But instead things got worse. Over the next 10 years she went on taking hard drugs, her health deteriorated drastically, and she had another child, who I'm also bringing up.

Social Services appointed a family worker for Lara. She was still in and out of hospital, with her breathing. The consultant had been telling her, 'Lara, sort yourself out – stop smoking, stop the drugs, otherwise you're not gonna see 30.' I still had Kelly. I was trying to get child care and stay in work, which was a nightmare. But at first we managed. Leanne's friends were brilliant cos they helped out during the day. Leanne were working by this time.

But then Lara began to disappear with Kelly, who were 3 now. She'd come back high as a kite, and Kelly'd come in, crying and filthy and literally starving. One day we'd been ringing round everywhere, but nobody'd seen them. We were beside ourselves. She turned up about 9 o'clock at night, completely off her head. Well Leanne flew at her and slapped her. I mean, we'd been absolutely going through the roof, wondering where the heck Kelly's gone. Has Lara collapsed somewhere? Is she left on her own? Lara went to bed and we sorted Kelly out.

But Lara ended up in intensive care again, with her breathing. Whilst she was in intensive care, I'd had to take a couple o' days off work to look after Kelly. And I were tidying up, and I found a letter from Lara's family worker to housing, stating that she was suffering domestic violence at the hands of her sister and her mother! Can you believe it? I were so angry. And whilst she were still in hospital she got a letter from the housing, awarding her a flat in Blackstone, which she accepted. I confronted the worker – 'You're saying she's suffering domestic violence.' She says, 'She is.' I said, 'Look, her sister slapped her. Lara came in, completely off her head. She's a drug addict. Drug addicts are brilliant liars. Lara has got a drug worker. You haven't checked it out with anybody. You've taken the word of a drug user.'

Well they said they'd allocate a different worker to Lara, and try to keep me more in the loop – but because of confidentiality... I said, 'She's got a child here. I need to be kept in the loop.' Nobody had thought how Lara would manage on her own in a flat with Kelly. She came out of hospital and got the keys. I thought, 'Delay tactics – try and keep Kelly here.' But she insisted on moving straight in, wi' nothing. I couldn't stop her taking Kelly.

Lara Moves Out

Every single night after work I were calling at Lara's, checking on Kelly. I were still having her every weekend, all weekend. I were getting phone calls from so-called friends of Lara's to fetch Kelly – 'We've had to ring an ambulance for Lara, she's gone into hospital.' Kelly was about 3 then, but she wasn't at nursery because Lara wouldn't tek her – she couldn't get out o' bed to take her. You know, her own priorities were all that mattered. She were supposed to attend parenting courses and everything – which she didn't. She'd say, 'I'm not well enough to go and I can't get there.' So this family worker would come out and see her, once a week. I was getting told nothing whatsoever. I were still ringing up wi' concerns.

Kelly was quite a bright child for her age. One day they went to a shop, opposite where the flats are. There was a big queue. Kelly picked up a roll of tinfoil – this was before she was 4 – and she said, 'Mummy! Smokes, smokes – give her the roll of tinfoil for her [heroin] smoking!' And the girl who told me this said Lara just walked out. They were here one Saturday – when she were only 2 – she were watching a programme with Leanne – a children's programme where they were making stuff with tinfoil. And Kelly says to Leanne, 'Nana cooks with that. But my mummy smokes it!' Leanne nearly went through the floor. We had all that. So I'm still on the phone to Social Services. But they believed Lara. They were thinking I were deranged because Lara had told them, 'She's trying to steal my baby, because her son's died.'

Eventually Kelly got a school nursery place in an afternoon, because Lara didn't surface on a morning. But it wasn't compulsory, so if Kelly didn't turn up, it didn't ring alarm bells. She never did a full week. And the uniform'd be too small for her, other parents were talking. I got told this by one of her friends whose son also went to the nursery.

Meanwhile Lara would leave her with me for so long – I mean she once left her here for 4 months, never took her back at all – in 4 months! Lara had been in and out of hospital I don't know how many times in that 4 months. I said to her, 'Look. She's living here permanently, Lara, I want the family allowance. You're not paying anything for her. I'm having to pay for everything, meself. You shouldn't be getting that if I'm looking after her.' So she took her back again! At the end of 4 months she took her, because she didn't want me to get the family allowance.

I couldn't take me eyes off Kelly. Social Services said, 'We don't think there's concerns. All that we can advise you to do, if you think that you've got enough concerns, go for a Residence Order.' Of course that takes the onus off them, onto me. I says, 'But then you've got to do a report, so you are confirming that you believe things I said – but you don't believe us enough to do anything about it.' 'Well no', they said. 'Because lots of parents who are drug users are quite capable of still parenting.'

Getting a Residence Order

So I decided I were going for Residency. To cut a long story short, it took me 15 months of fighting through the courts. I had to go and get a solicitor. It cost me £2500. At first it was down at the county court. Lara only turned up in court three times and they wanted to adjourn the case for 6 months. So in the end my solicitor said, 'We're getting nowhere wi' this.' In the meantime they'd shown me the papers of Lara's drug tests. And 12 out of 13 consecutive drug tests had shown up positive. I said, 'And you think that's not a reason to proceed?' They'd also had a complaint from Lara's neighbours, saying that Lara was sending Kelly round saying, 'Can I borrow a slice of bread? Can I borrow a potato?' They said they were giving it to her, thinking at least it's for the child, not for Lara. And there were reports of Kelly being outside, on the corridor, at something like 2 o'clock in the morning. Men coming and going from Lara's flat all hours of the morning, shouting, carryings on. And I said, 'You don't think there's a problem?'

So anyway, my solicitor applied for a higher judge and we got a circuit judge who dealt with the drug dealers and the big scale. And on his first hearing the judge appointed me temporary custody. And they removed her from Lara at

2 o'clock, that afternoon. They had to get the police and everybody to do it, because Lara were kicking off and threatening to kill herself. She's not quiet. She shouts and screams and swears and everything. She'd run from her flat, with Kelly. She'd hidden herself in somebody else's flat, so the police were going round looking for her. They eventually got her into the police car, with Kelly, and they handed her to me.

Later the police said, 'Lara's got no money.' I said, 'She never has any money.' 'Will you just give her £30 to do some shopping?' I said, 'She'll spend that on drugs, and she will kill herself.' And they more or less said, 'Well, there's nothing we can do about that, just give her the money.' So I give them the £30. I said, 'You're asking me to do this', I said, 'I'm not doing this of my own accord.' And Lara rung up screaming – 'You give me money so that I can overdose! What sort of a mother are you?'

At the end of the court case I got awarded full custody of Kelly on a Residence Order, until she were 18. By that time Lara had convictions for theft and everything and they realised that everything I was saying was proved. But even after I got the custody she'd come home and demand money, and the police told me I had to give her money before she'd go. I said, 'But you're helping her habit.'

Somehow I still managed to hold onto me job, but how I did it, I just don't know. Leanne helped. The judge said Kelly had to stay in the afternoon nursery, but then I had to put her in another nursery in the morning because I was working full-time. Pick her up at dinnertime, and drop her down to the other nursery for the afternoon. For 12 months she was in two nurseries and I had to fund the private one. It cost me. But I literally managed, by the skin of me teeth. Kelly was as bright as a button at nursery. Of course she were always going up to complete strangers – 'Look what I've got' – sort of seeking attention. She were always full of life, to the verge of hyper, but she wan't too bad. So that went on for a year.

And then Lara disappeared for 6 weeks. It was lovely, absolutely lovely! But one day she came through the back door with an Easter egg for Kelly, who was about 5 by now. Then she said, 'Oh I got to go, somebody's picking me up' – and walked out the front door. It turns up that she's got a new boyfriend. He ended up being Katy's father. I only ever seen him twice and that was fleetingly. But one day we've come home from school and Kelly's said, 'Oh-oh, me mum's at the door.' He were beating her up. She'd turn up here with black eyes, cuts, bruises, cigarette marks, everything. I think there were a couple of miscarriages as well. She'd turn up in the middle of the night, knocking on the door to be let in. She turned up one night when she was pregnant, at 2 o'clock in the morning. And she'd walked from Greylington to here. He'd beaten her up. She could hardly breathe, she collapsed through the door. I rung the ambulance and they said, 'What's happened?' I said, 'She's asthmatic, she's struggling to breathe, she's pregnant.' 'How's she got like this?' 'Her boyfriend's beaten her up.' So they sent the police as well. She gave a statement to the police – and then afterwards withdrew it.

Another time, I were at work, Kelly were at school, and I got a phone call from Lara, screaming and shouting down the phone: 'Him and his mother have kicked me down the stairs, kicked me head in, me head's all bleeding.' And she said, 'I'm just covered in blood.' She were somewhere near the BRI [Bradford Royal Infirmary], so I said, 'Right, get to the hospital, I'm coming now. I'll get the police at the hospital.' I rung the police straight away. I rung the hospital to put them on alarm. Well, she didn't show up! She didn't turn up at the hospital. By this time I'm thinking, 'Oh my

God, she's dead in a ditch somewhere. She's collapsed.' The police were out looking. She were missing for a whole week! By this time she was on the Missing Person's Register. And the police had gone to *his* parents' house – he were missing as well. So they presumed that him and her were together, but they didn't know what state she was in, whether she were alive or dead. And the police kept getting in touch with me – 'Has she turned up?' 'No. Nothing.' I were beside meself. After a week the two of them gave themselves in at a police station – claiming I'd exaggerated and there was nothing wrong, though her head was injured.

A Second Child

Later they caught him beating her up at the hospital when she went in for detox, so Social Services began to get more involved. They didn't believe me, but they believed the hospital. They had this meeting that I knew nothing about. They told Lara if she stayed with the boyfriend, the baby would be removed at birth. So she said, 'Right, we're going to split up.' I rung Social Services and they said, 'Lara's told us that she's moving in wi' you now, but you didn't have time to come to this meeting because you were working.' I said, 'Hold your horses. She's not living with me. I knew nothing whatsoever about this meeting because I was never told, or invited to it.' I said, 'If I had been invited to it, I would have come.' So they said, 'Oh, right. So you're *not* going to be having her and the baby back?' I said, 'I've already got one child belonging to her.' So they said, 'Oh right.' So anyway, there was a meeting after Katy were born and for a while Lara went to me sister's. Then she got another flat, but me and Kelly were often looking after the baby because Lara were back on the drugs again. Kelly were 6 when Katy was born.

Soon the furniture in that flat had disappeared too. In her room there was one chair – that's all she had left. Social Services were saying, 'Yes, there's a problem, but it's workable. We're bending over backwards to try and keep 'em together.' Lara were still in and out of hospital, but this time more regular. In the space of 12 months, she'd had 13 intensive care admissions. Whilst she were in hospital, Social Services took Katy in their nursery, but not when she were out. So because I had Katy I had to get me own child care then. And by this time, I was having more and more care of the baby, because Lara was spending more and more time in hospital. Then she'd self-discharge and go down Moor End for drugs, get Katy, go to her flat, but turn up here when she'd no money. Stealing left, right and centre – from Kelly, from me – birthday presents, Christmas presents. This was the scenario.

I were getting phone calls at night, sometimes 2 or 3 o'clock in the morning from Lara's neighbours. I'd put a couple of them on alert and they'd ring me. There's an ambulance outside Lara's. I would have to get Kelly out of bed, we'd walk up together to get the baby (I don't have a car). Kelly often used to say to me, 'Let's go get Katy, because she's safer here.' When I used to go get Katy, Kelly'd be with me so she would see Lara kicking off, and see her hiding the drugs and stuff, and attacking me. Lara would do anything: hit, kick, anything to get money off me. Kelly was about 8 now and that's when her behaviour started to deteriorate – maybe because of what she was seeing.

As if things were not hard enough, Steve came out of prison and applied to the court for access to Kelly, with a view to getting her back. I couldn't believe it. By this time he had another girlfriend and all *her* children were in care. I got a summons to appear at court, and Cafcass [Children and Family Court Advisory and Support Service – officials appointed by the court to investigate child care cases] was involved. They came round to talk to Kelly – which I didn't want at all! She hadn't seen Steve since she was a toddler and she couldn't remember him. Lara had covered up his prison sentence by telling Kelly, 'Daddy's gone to live in a castle.' The Cafcass people asked her to draw two islands and put all the people she wanted to be with on one island and anyone she wasn't sure about on the other. She didn't draw her father at all, so the officer said, 'What about Daddy?' And then she drew him in a boat out at sea! Steve refused to do a drug test and lost the case, and we didn't hear from him again, which was a blessing.

Leanne had her own house by now, so it were just me and the two girls, as I had Katy nearly all the time. I had to stop work because Lara was in hospital so often. I were constantly getting called out of work to go up to the hospital. And all the complications of child care. I literally had to make the decision overnight – and I said, 'Look, I'm not doing me work right, I'm not looking after the kids right. I'm just permanently exhausted from going from A to B.' I said, 'I'm just going to have to leave.' When I look back, I'm thinking, how on earth did I find time to work as well?

Endless Crises

The next couple of years were terrible cos Lara tried to kill herself several times. The first time I were at Kelly's karate class with the girls. Lara were in intensive care, but had discharged herself. There was a phone call from Leanne's partner for me to get home: 'There's two black police vans outside your house. There's an ambulance and there's Lara, lying down on the ground, and they're kicking your door in.' The police rung me and they said, 'We've got your daughter here. She made a 999 call to say the children have been kidnapped by you.' I said, 'She's a drug addict.' They agreed they'd found drugs in her possession. I said, 'I'm not handing this child – Katy – over to her. She's not *fit* to look after her.' I struggled back home as fast as I could. I told the children, 'Someone wants to talk to me about Mummy.' The police were there but the children were used to seeing ambulances, with the 999, the blue flashing lights and the siren. And they've seen their mother being tekken in, practically unconscious. By now, the police had accepted that Lara's definitely not right, and they said they would take her home and get in touch with Social Services in the morning.

When I'd heard nothing next morning I went to Lara's flat. I had a key but I couldn't get in at first because her key were inside the door. Anyway, I managed to knock the key out and found her, unconscious. She were just sat in the chair, gazing at the door, cold. By this time she was on permanent oxygen for her breathing, but she had none. I rang 999 and a [paramedic] came and managed to revive her and we got her to hospital. She owned up that she'd taken heroin the day before, then taken 41 of this tablet, 17 of this tablet – a long list! Her mental state was bad. She said she could see people coming to her flat to kill her, so she were going to kill herself, before they killed her. She ended up in hospital for 2 weeks and assessed by a psychiatrist, but then they said she was fit to go home – to my home! They promised an Early Intervention Team and she came home.

We didn't think it was safe to have the children at home as well as Lara, so one of Leanne's friends took them. We fed Lara and she had a shower. One of my sisters offered to stay in Lara's flat with her. But then Lara went in the kitchen and all of a sudden she said, 'Ha! You think you're clever – I've done it again!' She'd got paracetamol out of my cupboard, and took an overdose. I rung the ambulance and whilst they were coming Lara's got a knife. She refused to go in the ambulance. I managed to get the knife off her – I don't know how. Eventually I got in the ambulance with her and left me sister to get the children back. Lara was delusional. Now she were saying she were going to get 7 years for murder and there were road blocks up because the police were looking for her. Anyway, they sectioned her, after tests showed that she had damaged her liver and kidneys with the paracetamol. She'd also hit a nurse. And the nurse says to me, 'Does she do this to you?' I said 'Yes'. 'In front of the kids?' I said 'Yes'. So all this got noted down. And now it was coming from other professionals.

But the family worker was still saying they would work at placing Katy back with her mother! I said, 'You will not.' I said, 'Two intentional overdoses and you're telling me you're going to put Katy back with her?' I said, 'No way.' I rung Social Services and asked for the manager. He advised me to do as I did with Kelly – go for a Residence Order. 'Oh no', I said. 'I need your back-up wi' Lara. She needs restrictions.' I said, 'Without you enforcing it, I can't do it.' So anyway we ended up in a right shindig. Eventually they suggested I go for a Special Guardianship Order and they put a proper social worker in. Kelly wasn't even on their books, which is crazy.

Katy would have been 3 and Kelly around 10 years old when Lara was sectioned. She was under the section for 6 weeks, and then they kept her voluntary, then they let her home to her flat for a weekend to see how she would cope – and she used drugs. I'd got her a new phone, a new sim card, with no drug dealers' names on it whatsoever. And still she managed to get hold of a drug dealer! Well, of course she denied she'd used, and they discharged her home with the Early Intervention Team and a mental health worker. One day, before I got the Special Guardianship, she demanded I give Katy back to her. I couldn't legally stop her but I said,

'No, you're not taking her. If you want her, ring the police.' So she bought two lots of paracetamol and went to her flat and rang me, 'Done it again!' She was taken into hospital and discharged again the next day. And I said to 'em, 'If you discharge her, she will do it again.' And she did. And she was back in hospital again – for 2 weeks this time. But they wouldn't section her this time because they said, 'She knows exactly what she's doing.' I think it were a power game she were playing.

Well she calmed down, and then Social Services put Katy on supervised visits wi' Lara at a Family Centre. Both of them were taken there and back by workers. I wasn't involved. I asked why Kelly was not included and they said, 'There is no Order in place for Kelly.' That meant Lara could see Kelly as much as she wants, on her own! I said, 'If you're giving supervised contact to one child then you're also giving it to the other child.' And Kelly hadn't seen her mother for a long period when she was sectioned and in and out of hospital – I'd kept the kids well away. So Kelly went a couple of times, but she didn't want to go every week. She was playing up by then and her behaviour were disturbed.

Meanwhile the family worker was preparing a report for the court, but she wan't supposed to be talking to me. Lara were getting worse. She were getting blood clots in her legs. She hardly left the flat except to get drugs and cigarettes and to go to hospital, where they fed her up. At home she'd live on cereal. And Social Services were at last saying that healthwise she's not fit to look after the children. They still turned a blind eye to the drugs. Mentally she were off the planet. She ended up in hospital that many times that eventually they said there's no more we can do for her. Lara was dying – so we were told. Eventually she were placed in a care home with 24 hours' nursing care. She didn't die. And that's where she is until now.

I think Social Services recommended the Special Guardianship because they wanted Katy off the books. And I wanted her here rather than go out to adoption. They agreed to pay this time. But when we were going to court, the social worker had to contact Katy's father's family, to give them the option of tekking her. It took three arranged visits to get them. They told them, 'We're going to give custody to the grandmother – anything you'd like to say? Would you like to step in an' tek her, because you are the father?' (even though he's not on the birth certificate, thank God!). 'No.' And they said, 'Do you want to know anything about Katy? Do you want to see a photograph of her? Do you want to know how she's doing?' 'No, no.' Didn't want to see a photograph, *nothing*. So the social worker says, 'Do you want to put in for contact?' 'No. No. The only way that we would get involved is if the grandmother says she didn't want her.' I thought – in a way they've done me a blessing. And I did get the Special Guardianship then and this gave me some security. I also got a financial award and it's now on its second year. But I'm expecting that to come to an end.

I can't forgive Lara for what she's done. She knowingly had two kids. I think Kelly were born to keep Steve out o' jail, which she managed for 2½ years. Neither father's taken any responsibility. And what those children have seen and gone through! With Kelly, not only did she know what was going on with her mum, Lara's friends also used drugs quite openly in front of her. They thought she were too young to understand. One day, when Kelly was only 3, Lara were in hospital and me and Leanne were over at Lara's flat. Leanne says to Kelly, 'Where's Mummy's smoke?' Kelly pointed to t'top of t'cupboard and Leanne climbed up and found this inhaler that Lara used for taking crack. She'd put foil on the top of it and put pin holes in the top. Inside it were all blackened with smoke. She must have thrown it on top of the kitchen cupboard. Another time, when Kelly were 8, we saw an ambulance flying down the road, and she said, 'Me mum's private taxi!' So of course she's been affected.

Growing Up

As Kelly and Katy have got older they have started to get more difficult. It's not surprising I suppose. Kelly's always wanted her own way and got aggressive if she didn't get it. And she were stealing money off me. I said to her, 'I shouldn't have to hide me purse, like I had to do with your mum.' That's stopped now though. Kelly's quite a tomboy. She's not into fashion. So long as she's got a pair of trainers, she's happy. But that'll probably alter as well. At school every single teacher says the same thing. That if she could get marked on talking her way out of stuff, she'd be top of the class. She has calmed down a bit, recently. I mean she carried on this last weekend, but, up to that, for the past few months she has calmed, to what she was. I wa' thinking the other week, she hasn't really kicked off lately, where she's pushing or hitting me – which she did do.

But Katy now is doing it. And she is like a little terrier. She'll go for you. She'll bite. She'll kick. She'll scratch. She just loses it, instantly. And they can start with each other and end up shouting at me. Katy has got a Catholic worker for over a year now. The school pays for her to deal with any problem that crops up with a child. She's like a social worker, but she's under Catholic care. Katy sees her on a Thursday. Last week she had to draw a picture of her family.

Now the worker is supposed to be organising somebody to go into *Kelly's* school to deal with Kelly. Kelly gets *nothing*, no help at all. I was going to go for a Special Guardianship for her as well, and then I thought – what's the point? Lara's not gonna come out o' hospital and, heaven forbid, they'd never put the kids back with her. I freeze over to think of that. Kelly has probably seen Lara only three times this year at the care home – her choice. She says, 'Me mum's forgotten about me, so what's the point of going?' Katy has seen her mum more often, once or twice a month, and one day she actually put her mum some nail varnish on.

Meanwhile I'm still trailing up and down after Lara. She's still in the background, working everybody, even though now her lungs are ruined and she's been diagnosed with chronic obstruction pulmonary disease. The Early Intervention Team has pulled out now and she's with Community Mental Health, who expect me to provide for her 'needs'. If Kelly has a new pair of trainers, Lara'll say, 'I want some of them, get *me* some of them. I want a bracelet – I always wanted one of them. Get *me* one of them.' So 'Mum' is supposed to go out and get them.

I get scared in case Kelly or Katy goes the same way as Lara. Cos I'm thinking, God, two out of three kids! With Ben I blamed meself – I kept thinking I'd missed something, I've done something wrong. Ben was quiet and easily led. If only, I thought – maybe it wouldn't have happened. Ben did say to me, 'Mum, this was nothing that you did. It wasn't your fault.' And then Lara! Once Lara said, 'Ben were on drugs too – and that were all right with you.' I said, 'No it wasn't all right, Lara. But we have not had to say to any child of Ben's that your father died because he took drugs. Whereas with you we have to.' You know – her own brother died! I'm thinking, 'How could she?' Now I'm quite hard on Kelly. When she was 13 she was saying, 'Why can't I go to the cinema with friends on a night?' I said, 'Cos you are not going into town, on your own, with your friends – end of story. It's not *you* – I don't trust *other* people. I've been down that road with your mum.' Of course she says, 'Just because me mum does it, doesn't mean to say I'm going to do it.'

Having said all that, there's no way I'd be without 'em. You know, just no way on earth would I want to see them adopted – even sometimes when I'm at the end of me tether, and I'll think, 'Oh for God's sake, somebody just tek 'em!' – you know, I would not seriously turn round and say I can't cope any more. This year we went to Ireland with my family. That were nice – showing 'em, where my roots are. And they loved that. I really am proud of them, the way they've turned round. Kelly is stopping doing stuff, and I need to keep her on track, for her own good.

Looking Forward

I'm 61 now. I've got to wait for me pension until I'm 67! I don't qualify for the free bus pass either until I get me pension. There's still a mortgage on the house, but I do have the Special Guardianship award – and I also have control of Lara's money – though she doesn't get a lot now. Rightly or wrongly, I dip in and out of that for the kids and other expenses and to get what Lara asks for. I've got arthritis and I do struggle, bending and getting up and down. But I don't dare tell the doctors that. I don't want anything to be jeopardised. By the time I've got them to bed in an evening – and Kelly, as she's getting older, goes to bed later and later – by the time she's in bed, I'm fit for dropping. But I suppose I'm getting older – it's scary. If anything happens to me, the kids'll go to me daughter, Leanne. She said she would and I've made out me will.

I've no social life whatsoever – apart from Katy's school disco coming up in a couple of weeks – I'll get to chat with the parents! That's it, now. I've lost touch with all me friends that I had. They're all busy, and their lives are still going on. Sometimes they ask if I want to go out with them and I have to say I can't. Even though Kelly is old enough to babysit, they'd kill each other! The only person that I would leave 'em with is Leanne and her husband. If they're going somewhere with their friends they'll tek them out for me. They're good like that. The rest of me family tried to help, but I don't get on with one of me sisters. She never believed that Lara was on drugs, because Lara and Steve never actually did anything in front of her. So she'd no reason to suspect her. At one time she said, 'How can you kick her out?' I says, 'Because she's doing drugs, and she's stealing.' 'No she's not', she said – and she put the pair of 'em up – until I found a stash of drugs hidden down the side of the chair and she realised it were true.

I go to church. And the Catholic Church has got rehabs all over the country. The nuns attached to the church offered to put Lara into rehab for me when Katy was tiny. But Lara refused – she said, 'I haven't got a problem.' They even said, 'Look, Lara, you could go in with or without the baby.' But she said, 'I don't need them, I don't have a problem.'

The Grandparents Group helps though. I rung the Bridge Project years ago, when Ben was first involved in drugs. And I went a couple of times and they actually showed me how addicts injected and what they did – which I found it useful. But then I think things were just so chaotic, I'd stopped going. But then I had a feeling Lara were on crack as well as heroin – and I rang up just to see what the tell-tale signs wa', behaviour-wise. I began to see Mary, one to one. After Ben died things were still raw. Things can still be very, very raw. Just for no reason it hits you, even 14 years down the line. Mary said, 'Do you want to come to the group?' And at first I'm thinking, 'I don't really need this.' And then I went. I met Emma and her husband and I remember thinking, they looked normal – they just looked like a normal family – and yet they've got the same problems! So then that's how it began. Mary's good and I think to be honest, she's learnt an awful lot through it too. I mean there were probably a lot that she didn't know, that she's found out from different people. But when you get new members, I'm always a bit... wary, and you have to tell your story again. Obviously the longer we've gone on, we've all got that bit closer. And it's just like a family now, you know. I try to avoid missing.

* * *

Editorial Commentary

This is a complex account with many twists and turns highlighting many of the issues discussed in Caroline Archer's Afterword. The grandmother is struggling to manage two traumatised children, after already suffering the loss of her son to a heroin overdose. Drugs are like a cancer, spreading to the vulnerable, whilst others manage to remain immune. Kathleen's elder daughter remains strong and provides invaluable help in supporting the family. Sadly, the younger teenage daughter was already using hard drugs when her first baby was born. The baby spent 10 days in the traumatic environment of a neonatal care unit then went home to a chaotic household where drug use was normal.

A long-term pattern of 'revolving-door' care followed. The child would be 'dumped' at her grandmother's house without warning and without agreed length of stay, putting major strains on Kathleen as she attempted simultaneously to juggle the unpredictable demands of child care and work, to support her daughter and manage her own growing anxieties. The birth of a second child by another 'disappearing' father added to the crises. Kathleen's daughter was by now demonstrating serious mental health issues, threatening suicide and experiencing the long-term health effects of heavy drug use, leading eventually to her permanent hospitalisation. Like many working grandparents, Kathleen was forced to give up work.

Throughout, Kathleen was unable to access even basic support. Neither the police nor Social Services would at first act on her concerns about her grandchildren. She was excluded by confidentiality rules from accessing information that might have allowed her to intervene more effectively. She was not believed, and the rights of abusive parents were given precedence. She was forced to pay legal costs in order to get a Residence Order to protect the first child, and she has to carry all the financial costs of bringing up two children – on top of dealing with continuous crises generated by her daughter's behaviour.

Here, again, we see a violent, addictive and vindictive father allowed to demand legal access to his child and threatening her security. But Kathleen's bond with her daughter remains potent, despite the substance abuse, the denial of responsibility, the violence and demands for money to support the habit. These grandparents do not give up on their adult children or their grandchildren, though in this case the willpower required to be an active participant in removing the grandchildren from the abusive care of their parents should not be underestimated.

The grandparents cannot, however, undo the damage that has already been done. Drug use causes neurobiological damage to unborn children. Furthermore, violent interactions with parents using addictive substances, and who provide little basic security and neglect their children's basic needs, are traumatising for young children. They continue to carry with them the horror of these early traumatic experiences and, in this case, both display 'acting-out' behaviour – typically striking out at those with whom they feel safest. As the children grow older the future is uncertain, but Kathleen's consistent care is making a difference and they are settling down. Eventually Social Services gave her the support to obtain a Special Guardianship Order for the second child.

Like other grandparents, Kathleen fears dying before the children reach independence. Her older daughter has come forward to offer help, but this is not always possible. Grandparenting the children of substance abusers has a profound impact on grandparents' lives. It is an intensely isolating experience, especially for parents who 'don't have a clue' about drugs and know no one else in their situation. Shame can compound fear and paralysis, leading them at first to hide their concerns. When they do speak out, they are often disbelieved. They lose friends, work and the time or resources to rest or socialise. This is why the self-help group can be so important – becoming, as Kathleen says, 'like family'.

4

Amelia

'We've got to break that cycle'

Amelia took on her grandchild, Jason, 8 years ago when she was 65, and a year after she split up from her husband. Amelia's daughter, Jessica, and her partner, Ryan, had badly neglected the child.

* * *

I don't know at what point Jessica started taking heroin, but Jason was only a little tot. And she put him through so much hell – how could she do that? Can you imagine living with two people, shouting and bawling and banging until the early hours of the morning? Not feeding him properly? And then you see, they wouldn't wanna get up until midday. And then it'd all start again. It must have been terrible for him. You're upset, because you're thinking to yourself, you know, how *could* your daughter do this to her own child? How *could* she? I mean, you know you're not perfect yourself: when you look back you think to yourself: 'Well, I wan't a perfect mother meself.' Perhaps some things I could have done different. But I didn't neglect Jessica. You just can't get your head round it. I couldn't let him go through it. I knew he wouldn't be safe.

But what 65-year-old woman wants to start again? At my age I wan't going to *choose*! I mean I just got rid of a flipping nasty husband 12 month before! I left him to get a peaceful life. So I didn't *choose* – it wan't my *choice* to have Jason. I had 12 months of freedom. Then your life sort of stops, doesn't it? I had a social life. I used to go out wi' me friends. We used to go on holiday together; we used to go abroad together. There were six of us, all women. I could go out for t'day, just go out. I didn't have to bother about asking anybody. But now you can't – cos you're watching the clock all t'time.

You're called a grandparent, but you're not. A grandparent is someone who has 'em for the weekend, has 'em for a week in the holidays, spoils 'em. I can't do that. No matter how you feel, how ill you feel, you've got to get up, out of that bed in the morning, you've got to get him to school. You've got to bring him home, you've got to make sure that everything's okay, you've got to make sure you go shopping, you've got to have things in, you're thinking all the time, 'This has got be done, that's got to be done.' You can't just get up and think, 'I'm just gonna do nothing today, have a day in bed.' Not that I've ever been one to have a day in bed! I'd think that'd be very boring! But you know what I mean? You can't think of yourself. You've got to think of him.

Jessica was a lovely girl when she were a toddler. But then she turned into a rebel. She's always been a rebel. When she were younger, she were running away from home when she were 14 and 15. I were bad with me rheumatoid [arthritis] and I could hardly walk. But we used to go to Morecambe to pick her up; we've been to London to pick her up. When she was 16 she said, 'Kick me out and I'll get a flat.' She'd have her own freedom. I said, 'You won't get a flat as easy as that! And with a flat, Jessica, comes responsibility. You're not even working.' But then she seemed to settle down a bit until she met this lad, Ryan, who were an alcoholic. Why do they always meet these people? She's a nice-looking girl, she had long dark hair – she could have had the pick of anybody! But she picks these losers, none of 'em work. But she's quite happy.

And then she and Ryan got together and they got a place to live and had Jason in 2004. She really wanted a baby. They went in for a baby. And I knew that Ryan was a full-blown alcoholic. I knew that Jessica drank a lot – she drank more than what I thought she should drink – but that could be just a mother thing. And I knew she was a bit nasty in drink – although I didn't for a minute think she was ever cruel to Jason, because I'd never seen any signs that she had. She'd packed in drinking and smoking when she were pregnant. She did spend a lot of time with me and when she was with me, she didn't smoke or drink. And in fact when Jason was first born, she didn't want Ryan around, but he said, 'I've cut down, and he's my son, don't take my son away.' I don't know whether *he* was on drugs at that time. Cos I were a bit naive actually. People seemed to know before I did.

As time went on, Jessica started drinking more. I'm not saying more than what she did before she got pregnant, cos she always drank a lot. And I used to see Ryan had a bottle of cider from the time he got up. And she was always coming to me for money – 'Well it's for Jason, you know, we need some food for Jason.' Or 'Jason needs this.' And of course when it's a child then you do help. But I played hell with Ryan. I says, 'Why should I give Jessica money, when you're drinking your cider?' 'Oh, I don't take no money off Jessica for my drink!' he says. I said, 'No, but you don't give her any!' Neither of 'em worked. They were both on benefits. And this went on for about 3 years.

And then I were on the phone to Jessica one day and he were *screaming*, was Jason. I says, 'What's up wi' Jason?' She says, 'Oh it's that bitch next door. She won't let Jason play with her girls and he always plays wi' 'em and I've got to keep him in.' And she says, 'I'm going to pay her back. I'm going to bash her!' I says, 'Don't! That's no way to go about it.' I says, 'You'll end up in trouble. You could go to jail and what's going to happen to Jason then?' And then Jessica come to me and says, I've got a letter from Social Services – she'd been reported for neglecting Jason. 'I know what it is', she says, 'It's her next door. She's always at me. She says I take drugs an' all sorts – but I *don't*!' And I said, 'Just because you drink, it doesn't mean to say you're on drugs.' An' afterwards I thought, 'How bloody stupid am I?'

She got a letter saying she had to go to see the Social Services. Jessica knew she had to be up there for a certain time, but she didn't get out of bed. She rang me up – 'Can you ring Social Services, and tell them that we slept in?' So I rang t'Social Services. Told 'em who I was, and I were ringing on behalf of Jessica. I said, 'Look, I don't know what all this is about, but I hope nobody's going to come in and just take that child off of her, because of the say-so of the neighbour that they don't even like.' She said, 'Look, we're not in the habit of just going in and taking kids off of their parents, without a reason.' She says, 'All we want to do is see Jessica, talk to 'em, see Jason and see that he's okay.'

Anyway, the social workers decided they'd go down to visit her at the house instead. And Jessica comes and says, 'Aw', she says, 'Can I have some food for t'cupboard? I've looked in me cupboard, there's no food in the cupboard.' And I says, 'You should buy food in for that child, before anything else. Always pay your rent and always make sure there's food in that cupboard for the child. Even if *you* go without' – cos I've had to go without, when she were little, many times. Anyway, two social workers went and they seemed quite happy. They looked at his bed – and as it happened she'd changed the bed. So that was okay. 'They seemed quite happy', says Jessica. 'They were all right', she said. 'All nice and friendly.' And then she says, 'That's one in the eye for her next door, in't it? I'm going to get her one night. She won't know what's hit her.' And I kept thinking to meself, 'Oh God', cos I knew what she was like. If she had a drink…

You could never get Jessica on the phone – unless she wanted something – and then I used to go down. And the curtains were always drawn. And I used to go in and say, 'Why is it dark?' She says, 'Well I don't want people looking in my window!' I said, 'The child needs sunlight! You can't live in t'dark!' And he'd get really excited to see me – his little hands'd be going like this and he'd be jumping up and down, 'Nana! Nana! Nana!' And sometimes if I were just going and just dropping summat off – it could be food, it could be her washing – I'd feel right guilty then. So there'd be many times I'd have him for t'weekend, I'd have him for t'week.

And she used to leave him with Ryan a lot. Now knowing Ryan, there's drink. And I'd ring her and ring her – and he'd answer t'phone, would Ryan. I'd say, 'Where's Jessica?' 'I don't know, she's not back yet.' 'Where's Jason?' 'Oh, I've got him.' So I'd wait a bit, I'd ring again. I remember this particular time, I rung again, 'Where's Jessica?' This was about 7 o'clock at night. 'She's not back yet.' So I *knew*, wherever she was, she was drinking. And I *knew*, that as soon as she got home, them two'd be fighting. So I said, 'I'm coming down for Jason.' I went down, and I took Jason home wi' me. The next day she rang me up, so I said, 'Well, where are you now then?' 'I'm at home', she says. I said, 'I expect there's trouble, last night then.' 'Oh yes', she says, 'I've got a bit of a black eye', she says. A bit of a black eye! I said, 'It's no good, Jessica, you just can't go on like this.'

When Jason were about 4 he was supposed to go to a mother and toddler group at t'church. Jessica told me it were £3 a time. So who give her the £3? Supposedly she took him twice a week. She took him once! They said, 'You've got to put his name down, and we'll get in touch.' But she never went back. And afterwards I found out it were free! I kept saying to her, 'Oh, did he like it then?' Cos he loved playing with kids – well they do, don't they? 'Oh yes', she'd say; 'he likes it – he's there from 9 till 12.' And I went down one day – there were nobody in at her house. I went to the church, and I couldn't find anyone. I called Jessica and she said she went for him early! And she never ever took him!

My friend told me something which really really upset me. Jessica and Ryan used to take Jason to the park in Westover, and my friend used to go with her two – she's got one same age as Jason, and she's got a son two years older. She says Ryan once came into the park with Jason. And she didn't know Ryan and he didn't know her, apart from seeing her in the park and Jason playing with her kids. Ryan says to her, 'Do you mind looking after Jason for half an hour while I just go to the shop?' Well, he didn't go back for 2½ hours! She were panicking. It come to 5 o'clock and she had to get home. She were ringing her husband at work and saying to him, 'What am I going to do? I've got this child here.' So her husband said, 'Look, all you can do, give it 5 more minutes and if he's not back, phone the police.' And, as it happened, Ryan come back. I told Jessica that he were 5 minutes away from the police being called, and Jason would have been taken into care *then*. Jessica didn't know anything about it, because Ryan didn't tell her. I said, 'You didn't even know who my friend was. She could have been anybody.'

And even then, I didn't think about the drugs – I thought it were all drink. By this time I'd left my husband, and I'd got a flat. And in August, when Jason were 4 and due to start school in September, I were going to America for a month, going to visit friends. Now Jessica kept on about her neighbour and how they were causing trouble outside, and the neighbour's brother threatened to put Jessica's windows through. And I thought all this is going on, and I'm going away. What's going to happen? So I says to her, 'I'm going away for a month. You and Ryan come and spend that month in my flat. By t'time we get home, it might all have died down. You know, you've had a month break.' I were stupid, but all I were thinking about were this fighting wi' the neighbours. If the police would have come they'd have took Jason there and then. I wouldn't be there to protect him. If it were just Ryan and t'neighbour, I would just let 'em get on wi' it, sort their own damned problems out. But when you've got a child there, and you're not there to protect 'em – I thought, what if they tek him into care? – you know, while I'm in America!

But then I found out, through *my* neighbours, what Jessica were like – knowing that her neighbour wan't really telling the lie about her. I kept getting texts from me friend who lived close by – 'All your neighbours are complaining about Jessica!' It were the worst holiday of my life! I just thought, 'Let me get home!' When I got home the first thing Jessica says to me is, 'Can Jason sleep at your house tonight?' And I says, 'I've just got home from holiday, Jessica.' 'But can he sleep?' So summat inside me said, 'Yes', and we brought a blow-up bed for Jason to sleep in. And then I went out and 'ad a word wi' me neighbour, and I says, 'What's been going on?' She says, 'Amelia, the shouting, the bawling, the falling out, until 4 o'clock in the morning! And Jason were screaming and running around outside, dirty and without clothes.' The neighbours wanted to complain to the council, but she told 'em, 'Don't. Wait until Amelia comes back and let her sort it out.' They took Jason and gave him a wash and got him some clothes.

And there was damage – Jessica said Jason had knocked over the flatscreen television and broken it. She said she had to put it out and somebody took it. She'd put me old television from the bedroom in here. And the bedroom wall was all holes – they must have been banging it.

Worse than that, Jason started school the week before I came back from America. Jessica and Ryan took him to school. Well he were sick, but they went home, went to bed and slept in bed all day. The child is ill and school couldn't get hold of 'em! I told Jessica I was not impressed at all. I said, 'I think I'll have Jason for a few days – you get yourself sorted out.' I went to school, told 'em that I were Jason's nan, and that he was going to stay with me for a few days. And they must have known there was summat wrong after that first week that poor child were there. I said his mum and dad's not right well, so I've got him. I didn't say it were drink – you don't say that to teachers, good God, no!

The week after, she come to me, and she'd had a drink. Jason were at school. And she says, 'Can you have Jason a bit longer?' I says, 'Yes'. Then she says, 'You know your television, that got broken – well, a friend of mine's mended it and he wants £100.' I looked at her and I says, 'I'm not bloody stupid – you told me it were broke, it couldn't be fixed!' 'Well, £50 then', she said. I said – 'You're getting nothing!' And you know, she turned really nasty! She went off in a huff. But then I had to go into town for something. And I had £20 in me purse. And I looked in me purse in the bank, and that £20 were gone. I felt sick. I rang her up. I says,

'You took £20 out o' my purse this morning.' 'I didn't!' says Jessica. I says, 'Jessica, I haven't got that much money that I don't know what I'm doing with it.' I said, 'You took £20 out o' my purse this morning.' So she says, 'Oh I don't care what you say, I didn't.' I says, 'But I know you did. *You* know you did. *I* know you did.'

Jason Moves in Full-Time

Anyway, this is September, and he's still with me. Jason's crying, 'When am I seeing Mummy?' But Jessica and Ryan didn't visit him. I said, 'If I'm going to have him, he needs his toys and more uniform.' I'd bought him all his school uniform, before he started school. Jessica said, 'I don't want to see Jason, because I don't want him to get upset. I'll leave his things in a black bag outside the door.' So that's what she did. And I've still only got a one-bedroom flat, wi' a double bed. So obviously Jason slept wi' me. And he were wetting the bed, sometimes three times a night. He stood there, half-asleep, crying, 'Nana, Nana, are you mad with me?' I says, 'No, Jason.' And then the bad dreams – he used to wake up screaming! He's so upset. And he were awful to sleep with – kicked, and his arm going out like that! I couldn't get no sleep. So I got rid of me double bed and I got the two single beds. I thought at least he can get his own bed. But even then, wi t'single bed, I'd find him in bed with me the next morning cos he just wanted that comfort. Or if he'd had a bad dream – 'Nana, I've had a bad dream' – I said, 'Well, all right, love.'

I still had it in my mind that they were going to straighten theirselves out, and have Jason back. We had to pass the end of his street every day to get to school on the bus. And every morning and every night, Jason would say, 'Mummy lives on there. Am I going to see Mummy?' I'd say, ''Course you'll see her again. She's not right good at the moment, but when she gets better...' I'd leave letters at their house: 'Jessica, what're you doing about your son? He's upset. He's crying all the time. I'm telling him you're not well.' Now and again, she'd ring me – 'How is he?' 'He's upset', I said, and I don't have any money to keep him on, only what I had. Social Services didn't know – it wan't official. And the thing is, I didn't want Social Services coming and saying, 'You're not fit to look after him.' Too old and I've got rheumatoid arthritis. I've had it since Jessica were 6 month old. I've had it over half my life. I'm not in the best of health. And I didn't want 'em saying, 'You're not well enough to look after him, we're going to have to take him into care.' When I *was* coping, no matter what the weather, I always got him to school. An' he were always clean, always tidy.

Anyway, Jessica promised to take him home by Christmas. And I said to Jason, 'Let's get a calendar.' We can mark off the days until he's coming home. We had it up on the wall, and every morning we'd cross another date off. And she did take him home for Christmas – 'for good' I thought. He had Christmas at home. On the 31st of December, she rang me. 'We're going to me friends today', she said. 'Can you have Jason, because I don't want to take him where we're having a drink and a smoke?' I said, 'Fair enough, I don't mind, it's New Year.' So I had him. Next day, I couldn't get hold of her – as usual.

Then it turned out that my ex-husband had called the police on Jessica! All this time Jessica's been going to her dad's and she's been stealing money off him. She told him she was on drugs. She said 'I know I'm taking money off you, but it's the drugs, you know – I can't help it.' He used to take her to t'bank, with him, because he walked with a Zimmer frame, and he'd draw out £700 at a time. With her there! She knew where it was. So to an addict – dead easy. I didn't blame him for ringing t'police in the least. 'I had to do something', he said, 'because she'd taken me money. She's just bleeding me dry.' She took advantage of him. He said, 'She's on heroin you know.' I mean – he just made it so easy for her! He put some money somewhere. And she took it. And he went back to where his money was and it wan't there. So he says, 'You've took me money.' She says, 'No I haven't.' So he took the key out o' the door and he wouldn't let her out. She must have pushed him on the settee, took the key and run out. So he rang his sister and they phoned the police.

I thought 'Oh God! What's going to happen now?' I asked my sister if she could do me a favour – 'Can you come and pick me and Jason up and let me come over to your house for t'weekend?' I wanted a breathing space. I wanted to think what I were going to do here. Cos I didn't want Jessica coming, getting Jason – cos she was supposed to come that night to pick him up – and going off, with the police looking for them. And they go on the run! All sorts of stuff, it does go through your mind!

I only stayed for t'weekend, and then I come back on the Sunday for Jason to go back to school on the Monday. Jessica rang me and I told her, 'The police are looking for you, Jessica.' 'Why is that then', she says. I said, 'Because you stole some money off your dad and you knocked him on the settee.' '*I did not!*' she said. And she were shouting over t'road, cos it was a phone box she phoned from – 'Ryan! Me dad's saying that I've stole some money from him.' And I can hear Ryan in the background saying, 'Oh, what! Next they'll be saying *I* did it.' I says, 'Look', I said, 'Jason's staying wi' me. You get this sorted out.' 'Yeah, all right', she says, 'it's better if Jason stays wi' you.'

So a few weeks go by. No word from Jessica. The police came to see me, and Jason's sat there, having his dinner. 'How are you Jason and how old are you Jason?' And he told 'em. They asked me, 'Have you seen Jessica?' I says, 'No. But she's telling me she were under drugs.' And the police officer says, 'Look. When people are stealing like that, it's for drugs. If she gets in touch with you, tell her to get in touch with me.' And she left me her card. Police have cards now! Anyway when it come to it, her dad dropped the charges. And Jessica rang up, just now and again – 'Is Jason all right?' I said, 'Have you been to t'police station?' 'Oh I've been to t'police station, I've sorted it out.' She were a liar – she hadn't been near t'police station.

I says, 'Look Jessica, I need some money really, I could do with his family allowance.' 'Oh well, I'm coming back for him next week anyway', she said. But she didn't. And I daren't ask for it again cos things got worse. The landlord evicted them because they owed a lot of rent and the house were in a mess. So then they were homeless. I din't even know where they were. She rang me up; she said she were in a tent somewhere. They were living rough. And one day they'd both fallen asleep: they've had a good bit to drink, and smoking their heroin an' all. And the tent caught fire! They could have been both killed. Just like that. But she happened to wake up when there was this smoke – she were lucky because I mean smoke can flipping kill before t'flames do! So they got out. They were going from pillar to post, sleeping on friends' floors and all over t'place. How could I even *think* to let Jason go? To that? I just couldn't. And then her and Ryan split up.

She did admit to me then that she was on drugs. She said, 'But it's all right, because I'm going to get clean.' I says, 'Are you going to go into rehab? Are you going to get help?' She says, 'Oh no, I can go cold turkey, it'll only tek a week.' I thought, 'Well that doesn't sound right.' So I rang up that helpline for drug addicts. It's in t'*Yellow Pages*, I can't remember what they call it now. I said to 'em about me daughter being on drugs, and she says she can cold turkey for a week. 'Is that right? Can they do that? They tell that many lies.' 'Not all heroin addicts tell lies', he said to me. I said, 'Right, well *she* does.' And anyway, he wan't right forthcoming. I just put the phone down on him, and I thought, 'Well, I'm no better off.'

Anyway I rang up again – I thought I might get somebody different this time. A really helpful man this time. He told me, 'Look, there's a place in Bradford – they call it Bridge. If you ring them, they'll give you a lot more information.' So I rang Bridge and they said, 'Look, we've got a lady who works for us called Mary, and she's dealing with grandparents. Do you want to come and speak to her?' I said, 'Oh yes, please.' What I wanted was to *learn* about drugs – whether what Jessica were telling me were the truth. I wanted in-depth information.

So I started going to see Mary, one to one. And Mary was saying to me, 'Have you thought about going for a Residence Order?' And I said, 'I don't know, Mary. She'll come back for him if she thinks I'm going to do that.' But I couldn't get no family allowance until I had a Residence Order because Jessica wan't going to give it to me willingly. So I'd have to put in for it and have it tekken off of her. And the tax credits – she was getting that – and she wan't going to give me that willingly. So the only way was to go to court – oh God, I were in turmoil! I couldn't *sleep*. I thought if she thinks I'm going for that she's going to come and get him. And what's going to happen?

In the end I did talk to Jessica. I said, 'Look, I've got to go in for t'Residence Order.' She says, 'You're taking my son away from me.' I says, 'I'm not taking your son away from you, Jessica, but the thing is', I says, 'I can't do nothing unless I'm his legal guardian. I can't do nothing with his school.' I said, 'God forbid, anything happens to him and he needs an operation or things like that. I can never get hold o' you.' I said, 'You've still got some rights. I can't take him out o' the country and I can't get him a passport or anything like that, without your consent.' So, Jessica hummed and haa'ed and then she said, 'All right then.' So I wrote her a letter, explained it all to her, I put it in writing so she could process it. It's not just like, she says summat and then I say summat and we both start arguing, and then she hangs the phone up on me, and we still don't settle anything. So I thought, if I put it in writing, and then she can process it herself, she can read it, perhaps two or three times, and she'll know that I'm not doing it to take her son away from her. I'm doing it for him.

Mary was a great help – she was marvellous. She got me some forms to put in for the Residence Order. She got me a family solicitor. She took me to the solicitor. She went in with me to see her. The solicitor were a nice lady. And she said Jessica and Ryan had to sign the form to say they were giving me permission to get the Order. And I said, 'You'll be lucky if you find her.' But they had a detective who finds people and she said, 'He's very good, he'll find her.' I says, 'He'll have his work cut out for him!' He could never get her in t'house. He's sat outside in his car for days at a time. In the end, though, we set up a meeting at the Tesco opposite the university, and they both signed.

I did get legal aid. If I'd have been working I'd have had to pay. So I was really lucky. We got a court date. That were nerve-wracking! You go to the new courts in Bradford – it's like going through t'airport, without going on your holidays! And Jessica didn't turn up – I *knew* she wouldn't turn up. The first time she didn't turn up, so they rescheduled it. And then, the second time the judge just put it through. He said she's signed it, and now I've got parental responsibility, so that I could apply for me family allowance and for the tax credit.

There's no money with a Residence Order – it's just a legal status – but she can't come and just take Jason. If she wants Jason, I could say to her that 'You can have him.' But it's a safeguard – if she comes and said that she wanted to take him out, and she didn't bring him back, I've got a piece of paper so I can phone the police. And I could have her picked up, which before, you couldn't. Before I got that, she could o' just come and tekken him – nothing I could do about it. This is why I didn't want to rock the boat too much.

I got the family allowance and tax credits then. I had to wait, but they backdated it to the time I applied for it, but they didn't backdate it the 12 month I had him before I applied. Because that's already been paid out anyway, to Jessica. I think that's wrong.

So all this time I'm coping with Jason. As a little boy, as a child, hisself – he were good, really. You know, he wan't a naughty child. But at school he'll sometimes cry a lot. And the headmaster says to me, 'What's happening?' And I said, 'Well, the thing is, I'm not quite sure – me daughter has got a problem, and I'm having Jason at the moment.' And I said to the headmaster, 'The Social Services are supposed to be keeping a check on Jason through school. Have they ever been in touch with you?' He says 'No'. Jessica'd been reported twice in 4 years and they don't even know he's living with me! They don't even know where Jason is!

At first I did honestly think it was only going to be for a short time. But as time's going on, an' the way she's acting, I think it's going to be longer. So I thought, well I'm going to have to find somewhere where he can have his own bedroom. And, as it happened, one of his school friend's mums had property she rented out and she said, 'We've got a house.' So I went to have a look at it. It were a new build, it were lovely. I said, 'Oh yes.' I thought, at least Jason's going to have his own bedroom. I don't know if he'll still end up in my bed!

So we moved into the house. But then me health deteriorated because of me rheumatoid arthritis. Me breathing got bad. I couldn't cope with walking downstairs, with me knees and back. I had to come out of the house because of me health. If I couldn't go up and downstairs it were no good to me, were it! Anyway the same lady had a bungalow for rent. After the house it seems so small. But anyway we moved in here. I've been here about 4 years now. I've got two bedrooms and I've redecorated it an' that, cos you've got to put your own stamp on it. Jason sleeps in his own bedroom now. He still has dreams now and again. He'll come in to me and he says, 'I've had a bad dream', and I'll say, 'Have you, love? Are you all right?' I get hold of him and hug him. I says, 'Are you all right', and he says, 'Yeah', and I say, 'Come on then, I'll put you to bed.' And I tek him back into his own bed. And he'll go back to sleep. He never says what the dreams are about – and by morning he's forgotten.

But then, you see, he'd got no friends round here. That's the trouble. In the holidays and that, I tried to have one of them here, or sometimes he went to their house. I used to feel guilty then, because wi' me being as I am, I can't always do things what younger parents do, because you just haven't got the energy. I mean, really he should have someone kicking a football with him and things like that. When we lived in the house there was like a medical centre in front of us, with a big car park at the side. There was nobody there at weekends, so I'd go and I'd kick a ball about with Jason. But I were rubbish! Here he mostly just plays at home.

When he was at primary, quite honestly I didn't really see the family allowance [she means child benefit, £82 a month], because it went on to t'bus fares tekking him to school and taxis. When we moved, I talked to Jason about moving schools as well, to be nearer home. But he got *so* upset. He says, 'Oh no', he says, 'I'll miss all my friends.'

And I thought, 'Well I don't want to uproot him, because he's already had enough upheaval in his life.' So I kept him at the school. Then I started to take a taxi because there's only 50 pence difference between a taxi and a flipping bus fare! I can't use me pass [senior citizen's free bus pass] – in the morning before half past nine. So I may as well get a taxi, and then I weren't rushing down the hill and rushing for buses in the morning.

Jason's 12 now and he's gone up to secondary. The school's back of me, here, and it's easier. Some of his friends from primary are there too, and he's got friends, he's popular.

An Attempt at Reconciliation with Jessica

All that time, Jason didn't have no idea what were going on with his mum and dad. How much do you tell 'em? When they're little, you can say to 'em, 'Well, your mum and dad's not well.' That's what I used to say to him. He has said, 'I'd like to see me dad', but it's 6 years since we've seen him. So I just say, 'Well we've never seen him love, so I don't know where he is.' And he can't even remember living with 'em. He told me he could remember his dad kicking the cat downstairs after it scratched him. But I think sometimes when things happen to 'em when they're young, they block it out. He might remember it later on, I don't know. And he kept saying to me, 'Where's my mummy?' And then he'd say, 'Is my mummy dead?' And I'd say, 'No love, she's not dead. It's just that she's not well and we haven't seen her for a bit.' Now I say his mum's just looking for somewhere to live, because this is the tale she's told us now. He didn't see her for 3 years after he came to live with me. And I only saw her once or twice – she asked me if I'd meet her and tek down some of her stuff I still had.

She got a one-bedroom flat then, near her dad. She come off the heroin and went on methadone. And then she worked herself down really low [reduced her medication]. She give me permission to talk to her key worker at Bridge. She said, 'I'm doing well, you can ring Bridge up every week.' But she was drinking far more than what she did. She was drinking more or less every day. She was getting money off her dad. Her and her dad used to fall out like mad, they were always arguing. She was supposed to do some housework to look after him and feed him. And now and again she went up and did it. But she knew she'd get money off of him. I says to him, 'You shouldn't give her money.' And he says, 'Well, I'm not as hard as you.' I says, 'But you're not doing her any favours. If she came here, I'd watch her like a hawk. Because you just can't trust her. Even Jason knows that she can't be trusted.'

Jessica still says she's getting him back at some point. She still does. To be honest, that would be the aim. I'm not going to live for ever. About 2 years ago she rang me one day, she says, 'I'm going off heroin and I'm on methadone, and I want to start seeing Jason.' I had a word with Mary and I says, 'I want to do this right, because he hasn't seen her for such a long time.' I says, 'I don't want him to start seeing her and then she loses interest.' So Mary, and meself, Jessica and her key worker started having meetings and we arranged it for every Saturday so that Jason could get to know her again.

The first time, we arranged to meet her in town outside Kentucky Fried Chicken. But you know, that first time Jason didn't recognise her! He remembered she had long dark hair, but when she stood in front of him and he looked at her he went all shy. And she says, 'I'm your mum.' So he says, 'I don't remember you.' And though she give him a hug, he took his time. We went in to Kentucky, where we had something to eat and he started talking a bit, but nothing much. When she's got up to go, he didn't cry. Then the week after he saw her again – and he did see her for a few weeks. But then she started missing. She wan't turning up, or she'd say she'd turn up, and we'd set off on a bus to meet her in town, and I'd get a phone call on the bus: 'Oh I'm not well. I haven't slept all night.' 'Jessica', I says, '*I* haven't slept all night, *I* still got to get up.' And then I've to say to him, 'We're not meeting mummy today.' 'Why aren't we meeting mummy?' 'Well, she's not well.' 'Well *why?* Is she – is she dying?' 'No, she's not dying.' You see, you've got all this torment. He's got all this inside! And you think to yourself, you know, what's she doing? And then she didn't see him again then till Christmas! And since then he's hardly seen her at all. If she rings she'll talk to Jason. He doesn't get upset now. He used to get upset when she didn't come. I suppose he's fallen into the pattern now.

But despite all she's done – he loves her! If he thought he wouldn't ever see her again...well, it's the thing that keeps him going I think.

Living with Jason

Because I've got the Residence Order, school knows I have responsibility. I think it's more or less accepted, even by his school friends, because I've always been the one that's had him, since a week after he started Reception. One day his teacher says to me, 'Look we know sometimes you struggle.' But they've got no reason to complain. He goes to school, he's smart, he's happy, he's well-mannered. Look at his certificate on the door: 'Star of the Week'! He is dyslexic, but he has come on. Since they found out – cos I asked for him to be tested – he's had one-to-one attention. They have worked really hard with him and he has improved. His last report from school – I could have cried when I were reading it – they said what a *polite*, well-mannered young man he's turning out to be. I was so proud. And they're saying his attitude is good – whatever it is he'll have a go at it. He's sometimes a bit uncertain, a bit slow, but they can see he's really trying hard, he's working. He's not one of these that won't. When he were little he were running around all over t'place, and I were a bit worried, in case he were like that at school. But I asked his teacher and she said, 'Oh no, once he's in school and he sits down at t'table, he does what he's asked to do.' He's always been like that. He's never been disruptive, he's very popular – he's got friends of both sexes, you know, girls and boys. And he does come out with the comicalist and funniest of things. Even when I'm feeling low he can make me feel good – he can lift my spirits – he can come up and give me a kiss or a hug.

Looking to the Future

I do worry about the future. When I've felt ill, and I've thought to meself, you know, I hope he never has to come into t'bedroom and find me. He got upset last week, saying he didn't want me to die. But I don't think it's something he dwells on in particular. It's just if summat triggers it off just now and again. As he's getting older, I teach him to use the phone. You don't have to remember numbers – he can scroll down to whoever he wants to speak to. He can do that. And I've always said to him, 'If ever you can't wake me up, or if I fall and I can't get up, ring somebody.' I once said to my brother, 'If I die, you won't see Jason going into care will you?' And he said, 'No', but he made a joke of it.

I can't believe Jason will have been with me 8 years. It's just flown by! I think this is it with Jessica – she's got that used to him being with me now and just popping up whenever she feels like it, saying, 'That's my son.' I can't see her having him back – not as she is now! She'd have to come a heck of a long way. She'd have to get somewhere suitable to live and be there for a long time and she'd have to *prove that she's changed*. I mean, it's not that long ago she kicked her dad! And he had bad legs. She didn't respect him, but he's never respected her either. I said, 'You reap what you sow. We've got to break that cycle.' Anyway, her dad died earlier this year and since then she's gone to pieces.

I've come to the conclusion that Jessica doesn't want responsibility. She'd have to get up in a morning, take him to school. He's got to be looked after, he's got to be clean, he's got to be fed, he's got to be loved, and not neglected. I don't think she wants that responsibility. And yet *she* will tell *me* that I don't live in the real world. I don't live in the real world! I says, 'I don't live in *your* world! And to be quite honest I wouldn't *want* to live in your world.' If you mention anything about kids getting hurt because of drink and drugs, she says, 'Oh I don't want to talk about it.' I says, 'No, you don't want to talk about it, but you don't mind living it!' She makes out to Jason that I was no good as a mother. 'Why do you tell him off', she says. 'Look', I says, 'I need charge of him, you know.' 'Oh but I know what you're like', she says. 'Sometimes you can be not a nice person', she says. I says, 'Well, you know, to say you know what I'm like, you didn't mind leaving him wi' me!' Then I got upset, one particular time, and I got upset in front of Jason, and that upset him – and I thought, I can't be getting upset, I got to control meself. But you can't afford to be too soft, bringing a child up. You've got to have a certain amount of discipline, because otherwise it's going to bounce back on you.

I don't know whether other people blame me for how Jessica turned out – I think everybody else can always live your life better than they can live their own. Until somebody's in the situation nobody knows what they'll do. But I blamed myself. I used to think, perhaps if I'd done this different, if I hadn't of stayed with Jessica's dad, would it have been different then? There's lots of things you can look back on and think, I should o' done that different. I've spoke to Mary about this and Mary says, 'You'd be surprised how many grandparents think that – they think they've gone wrong somewhere.' But Jessica could have had the most perfect upbringing and she could still have done the same things.

I am lucky really. Cos I've got me friend – and when I did go through a bad patch she'd come to take Jason to school. And me sister used to pick him up. If I ring her or me friend up and say 'I'm not feeling right good. Could you pick Jason up, or get me some shopping?' – they'll do it. It's *learning* how to ask. They do know that if I ask, I am desperate. I'm not taking advantage. And then there's The Grandparents Group. That's been good. If I can't make it, I do feel a bit sad. It helps because no matter how good your family or your friends are – and you find out who your friends are! – we all know exactly what each other's going through. People can only sympathise or empathise, but they don't really know how we feel. They don't know that feeling of your daughter or the son not being able to look after their kids – whether they can help it or they can't help it. Nobody knows what it's like. So I am *very* lucky.

* * *

Editorial Commentary

In the Afterword, Caroline Archer distinguishes two typical responses of children to childhood trauma: 'acting-out' behaviour (tantrums, hyperactivity, sleep or eating problems, lack of cooperation, impulsivity, destructiveness or aggression) and, less frequently, 'acting-in' (compliant, quiet, helpful, withdrawn). This account describes a child who has responded to the loss of his parents to alcohol and hard drugs, and their neglect and failure to protect him, with quite marked acting-in responses. What is clear is that his reactions are built on deep fear of further separation and loss, underlined by his mother's inability to commit to him and her short-lived reappearances in his life. Yet, despite his mother's behaviour, he still loves her and expects her to reclaim him.

In reality it is his grandmother's loving attachment and care that is crucial to his survival and with it he has made strides – enjoying friends at school, learning to cope with change and doing well with his school work. She is his comfort when his mother continually lets him down, and he is gradually acknowledging and coming to terms with his mother's untrustworthiness and inability to be the parental figure he needs.

Once again, the grandparents' perceptions resonate with the children's traumatic responses. Grandparents too are consumed by fear, shamed into silence and torn by conflicting loyalties to adult children and grandchildren. These fears are not irrational – social workers have the power to remove children; teachers may judge harshly; police may overreact. Yet, simultaneously, the drive to protect their vulnerable grandchildren requires grandparents to risk these distressing outcomes.

The cost is huge. Like other grandparents, Amelia emphasises that taking on a child was not her 'choice'; rather, it was a driven and loving duty. There is very real material hardship here because no financial support is available – even retrieving the child's support benefit and tax credits is not automatic, and risks confrontations with an already accusatory daughter.

Eventually this grandparent was able to battle through and get help from the drug rehabilitation service (Bridge), who offer far more than bald information. Their approach to support demonstrates that for services to succeed they should stand alongside families in desperate need of understanding and provide appropriate direct assistance, for example, when facing challenging ordeals such as taking legal advice and going to court. They can link invaluable one-to-one counselling with collective support, where meeting with others who know what it feels like to have children misusing drugs or alcohol, and taking on their grandchildren, can be infinitely comforting and empowering – particularly at a time when grandparents are feeling their age and perhaps becoming infirm.

5

Emma and Martin

'There's always this fear'

Emma and her husband Martin (both 60) have shared the care of their youngest daughter's three children since she was drawn into drug addiction and subjected to abusive relations with two of their fathers. They brought up the eldest, Lizzie, from babyhood to adolescence. All the children have now returned to their mother, Heather, as she has come off drugs. This is Emma's story, with Martin's help.

* * *

Lizzie was 18 months old before we realised anything was amiss. Our youngest daughter, Heather, was working full-time in a call centre and had been living in a small terrace house with Lizzie's dad, Matt. She was paying rent to us because we'd used nearly all our savings to buy the house for her. The relationship with Matt only lasted until Lizzie was about 4 months old. Then she was on her own.

At that point Heather was still only 18. She was a brainy girl, but she was pregnant when she was doing her GCSEs, expecting Lizzie. She still got 10 subjects. She's always been a rebel. She ran away from home when she was 12 and then half the time when I thought she was going to school she was truanting. I never knew at the time. What I did get to know was when she was pregnant. I got a call from the RE teacher who also did welfare, and Heather had been to see her. She was only 15 and she had a termination. I feel that all her life she's blamed me for that termination – everything's been my fault ever since, even though I told her, 'You don't have to do this if you don't want to, we'll cope.' And then 5 months later she was pregnant again! I kept it from Martin for 3 days. And when I told him she were pregnant again, it broke his heart. That hurt me more than anything. I said, 'She wants to keep it.' Then I had to tell the family she was pregnant – you know, Catholic family, can you imagine it? But they were supportive, especially Martin's mother, bless her – who at that point would be 70 – she just said, 'Well. Babies bring love.' That was all we got off her. No recriminations, nothing – we'll manage.

We thought we were managing. Martin took early retirement on health grounds and, once Heather seemed to be settled with her job and the house, we went for 6 weeks' holiday to Australia for our silver wedding. When we came back, Kay, my middle child, expressed some worries about Lizzie. She'd been up to Heather's and the house had gone from being reasonably well looked after to being dirty and a mess. She went up one day and it was 3 o'clock in the afternoon, and Lizzie wasn't dressed – she were still in her bedroom, obviously wearing the same nappy that she'd had on all night. Kay grabbed some clothes and took her to her house and kept her overnight. When we got back Heather tried to put us off going to the house and we couldn't understand why. But eventually we went – and one of the doors had a fist mark in it, the windows had been broken in, and the back door – she said she'd had burglars. I believed her, because I didn't have any reason not to believe her.

Drugs and Chaos

Nearly a year went past without us realising what was going on. Lizzie was about 18 months old by now and we were picking her up in a morning and getting her ready for nursery. Sometimes Heather worked late, so we would pick Lizzie up from nursery, feed her and then we'd get her ready for bed or we'd take her round to Heather's and we'd put her to bed. And Martin would go and pick Heather up from work and I would babysit. Can you imagine all this going on! And Martin wasn't 100 per cent well himself.

Every time we went to Heather's there was never anybody there except her. But, unbeknownst to us, she was cohabiting with a chap that used to go to school with her. He was the one that got her into the drugs. I never clapped eyes on him. I think he met her somewhere and in the course of the conversation she said she had her own home and she had a little one, and whether he saw her as an easy touch…? We were off in the caravan one weekend and she rang us and said, 'Can you come home, I need help – I need help!' So we went back and picked her up and said, 'What is it?' And she said, 'It's drugs. I'm taking drugs.' It floored me. I was clueless. I didn't know anything about drugs. It could have been cannabis or anything. I just didn't know. You just knew the word 'drugs'. So, we took her to the Bridge Project. One of the workers, who was very informative and very good, said, 'We'll try and get her involved in things here whilst she seems to be willing to do it.' And at that point Heather seemed to take it on board. I think the lad she'd been with was frightened off by Martin, cos at one point he was there and the next minute he'd blown.

A year went by and Heather seemed to be engaging at Bridge, though we knew things weren't right. Lizzie was about 3½ by now and we were looking after her most of the time, but Heather would come and say, 'I want to take her home. I'm taking her for a while, I'm just going for a walk with her.' We were worried but we couldn't stop her cos we didn't have a Residence Order. One Sunday morning Heather turned up, Lizzie had been with us: 'I'm taking her out.' Well, it was throwing it down! 'You're not.' '*I am*, you can't stop me' – and she ended up calling the police, cos we wouldn't let her take her! At this point she was using Lizzie as a shield – she had Lizzie in her hands, she was physically pushing Martin away, and...it was horrible. The police came, and a policeman took us in one room and a woman took Heather in another. At the end of it all they said, 'Have we got a Residency Order or anything?' The answer to that was no. Well you've got to let her take the child where she wants, cos she's her mum. And she took her. It was horrible! I felt so ashamed. I were heartbroken.

My eldest daughter, Marie, was getting married soon after. I was trying to put a brave face – I couldn't tell her all this was going on. Heather took Lizzie on the Wednesday, and she didn't bring her back until the Friday! And we'd no idea where they were. I didn't tell Marie she was missing. I got the police involved, because I thought, 'I don't know where the child is' – I was worried for her safety. But the answer that I got was: 'Well, she's the parent, but we'll put a lookout on and see if we can see her.'

Marie and Steve were getting married on the Saturday. We went to the wedding rehearsal without Heather, or Lizzie, who were both bridesmaids. I said that Lizzie wasn't very well and Heather was looking after her. I didn't tell Marie that they were missing. I think she had some idea, cos we both looked dreadful, but we went. I even rang the priest up, and explained to him what was going on, so that he didn't inadvertently say something in his sermon. I had to explain to him it wasn't quite as straightforward as a normal wedding and that there would be...undercurrents. He was super, he really was. But I also had to explain that she was missing and I didn't even know if she might turn up in the ceremony.

Anyway, she turned up on the Friday, the day before, wet through, with Lizzie totally wet, dripping wet. I just said to her – 'Don't talk to me. I don't want to talk to you, just go upstairs, get in the bath and put Lizzie in the bath.' And I made Lizzie something to eat. I was so relieved to see them. But at the same time I was *so* angry with her. I said, 'You spoil your sister's wedding tomorrow and I'll never speak to you again. Ever.' That was it. I said, 'I've done with it, I've had it.' At that point I could have – really, I could have killed her myself! You know, all this money! And the wedding was supposed to be such a lovely, caring – and everybody was ringing up, 'Oh it's going to be lovely' – and I had to pretend everything was fine.

Anyway, Heather was fine the morning of the wedding. I got the two little bridesmaids ready, and then I got ready in 10 minutes to go to her wedding. Nobody knew, not a soul knew, that Heather had been missing that week. I'd not told anybody, any of my sisters, I'd told them nothing. All that day, I was on edge. And it got to the evening, and it was obvious to us that she'd used something – she suddenly went hyper, and you know... But whether it was obvious to anyone else I've no idea. Everybody else was wrapped up in what was going on.

That was the first time, I think, that I felt anger towards her. She'd let us down *so* much. Every time it was, 'I'm going to do something about it', but she didn't. Instead she'd let in another bloke, Des, who seemed perfectly all right on the outside, but again, he was another user. She lived about a mile away from us, on Highfield Road in Weirfield, and the police were there so many times. This is it – I mean everybody knows. Everybody knew that the police were outside her house, nearly every other day.

By now I had real concerns about Lizzie going back to Heather's house. The health visitor was due and Heather said, 'Can I ask her to come to your house?' She didn't want the health visitor to go to her house. It was actually the same health visitor that I'd had, so I rang and said to her, 'You know, I've got concerns.' She said, 'Well, the best thing you can do is to persuade her to let you have Lizzie on a Residence Order.' At this point I'd also rung Social Services, asked for someone's advice, and that was exactly the same. 'If you've got concerns about the child, you need to get a Residency Order.' It was unbelievable. You don't even know what a Residency Order is!

When the health visitor came for the assessment, Heather broke down and said, 'I need some help, because I can't look after her.' The health visitor said, 'Well, why don't you let your mum and dad look after her, for a while?' And Heather looked at me and I said, 'Yeah we'll look after her for a while.'

Mind you, I was still working then, part-time. Martin wasn't working. I was working as a medical secretary. We were paying for Lizzie to go to the nursery, so we could manage. Heather agreed she would think about this Residency Order, so I contacted a solicitor. She said, 'If you want to go for a Residency Order, you need to do it now, whilst she is in agreement, cos if she changes her mind it's going to be more complicated.' So that's what we did – we went to court, and the first time, the judge threw it out because Lizzie's father, Matt, hadn't been informed.

Matt was seeing Lizzie once a fortnight. He's never been involved with drugs or anything, so I had to ring him and tell him that Heather was a drug addict. The shame of it – that were awful. Telling him that we were taking on looking after Lizzie…I was so fearful that he would say, 'I want her.' Matt is a nice man, he's a lovely man, but at that point he was in a relationship with another woman. Lizzie didn't like this woman – and it was pretty obvious that *she* didn't like Lizzie. Anyway it didn't come to that, because he never offered. But he did pay us a little bit of maintenance. For the first year or so, he did give us a little bit of money, every month. Then his partner became pregnant, and so it was halved. I can't remember what he gave us – perhaps about £60 a month. From his salary that was a lot.

Matt took her one night a fortnight, so we got a night off. His parents were divorced, and both remarried, but they kept in contact with Lizzie as well. His dad, particularly, used to ask us – could he have her for the weekend – and they took her to Euro Disney, and they also took her to the pantomime every Christmas. They did things like that with her. Sometimes I used to feel that they got the fun bits and we got the care, because during this time Heather was chaotic. We decided to move house. I couldn't bear the neighbours and everything…and all that had gone wrong. We bought a small bungalow and we were having a lot of building work done. One day, the builder, who was a good friend, left his phone and we rang him up to tell him. Heather appeared for an hour that night and then we couldn't find the phone anywhere. We had to ring him up and say we thought we'd thrown it out by accident – making excuses for her! But it was obvious she'd pinched it. We'd so many things go missing, and she'd say, 'I am so sorry, I'll save up and get you a new one.' We bought Lizzie a karaoke machine one Christmas, and Heather asked if she could borrow it. We never got it back. But like idiots, I didn't want to think it of her, that she were stealing from us.

But we decided at that point that that was it – we wouldn't keep Heather's house on any more. We sold it and used the money for work that we needed doing in the bungalow. Heather went and lived with Des. Because of the Residence Order application, we had Social Services coming to see whether we were fit people to take on a child. It was horrendous! I said, 'I've looked after this child more or less since she were born. And now you're coming to see if I'm fit' – well it just has to be done. Of course, they needed to see us with Lizzie, to make sure we were responding to her – I felt as if I was having to prove meself. It was ridiculous. Just one visit though, for an hour.

Lizzie was very settled with us – just a normal baby, too young to realise what was happening. At first she'd go off with her mum and come back, and she missed her mum when she wasn't there. When she got a little bit older and I'd say 'Mummy's coming', she'd stand at the window looking for her. But Heather often didn't come. I remember one day in particular when we lived at the bungalow and she promised Lizzie she'd come to take her to the park. I said, 'Well I'll come with you to the park' – I was so frightened she'd disappear with her. This was before we had the Residence Order. Well, Heather didn't turn up. Lizzie kept looking out – 'Is Mummy coming now? Is Mummy coming now?' I said, 'She's coming at lunchtime.' And Lizzie kept saying, 'Is it lunchtime?' And 12 o'clock came, and 1 o'clock came – so I said, 'Shall we have a pretend picnic?' I made a joke of it, tried to take her mind off it. And she just looked at me and said, 'Mummy's not coming today, is she?' It broke my heart – because this was a 4-year-old child.

At one time Heather took her back to a flat she lived in. This was before the Residency Order came. She'd put a picture on the wall in the bedroom – it was teddy bears – and Lizzie just sobbed her heart out. That picture must have had horrific memories for her – maybe it was all she could see when she'd been left in the bedroom a long time – but anyway, the picture was thrown away, by me. I said she doesn't like this.

We got the Residency Order the second time we went to court, because Matt had written a letter saying that he didn't have any objection. Once we'd got the Residency Order we never saw sight nor sound of Social Services again – any of them. We've never had another call from them. That was it, nothing. Now Lizzie didn't go back to Heather's. She stayed with us. Heather'd come and she'd take her out or come and see her. Or she'd come and stay a couple of days. We'd got the Residency Order; that was that.

But Heather herself were chaotic. The police were knocking us up, 'Is Heather, your daughter, here?' They searched the house, even Lizzie's bedroom. She was giving our address as a bail address whilst she's not here. They never told me what she was on bail for, and Heather never told me. Handling stolen goods, I think.

The new bloke, Des, was using still. Then she was pregnant to him and she had a termination and their relationship fizzled out. We took her in with us in the bungalow. We thought she was trying to come off drugs. Lizzie thought this were great – her mummy upstairs. She'd go up every morning and wake her up. But I went up one day and I found these little white things on the floor and I thought, 'What are these?' I'd no idea what they were. Then I started looking at them and I'm suspicious. I asked Heather – 'What's all this?' 'Oh I've had a biscuit…' And then I found a hypodermic needle in the bed where Lizzie got in for a cuddle. I still *had no idea*. Then she admitted to me that she was taking heroin. She told me that she was injecting it and I was more horrified.

The police came one night, for whatever reason, but she'd gone and she'd not come back. But we had the Residence Order so we still had Lizzie. One day we were supposed to be going on holiday with my sister, and Lizzie was to stay with her auntie Marie. Heather turned up. She told us we couldn't go because *she* wanted to take Lizzie for the weekend. And there was all this screaming and shouting. A few days later Heather stayed and bathed Lizzie. She said something to her which hurt me terribly – 'Oh they don't really love you. They just want you cos they don't want *me* to have you.' At that point I said, 'Just go, Heather.' It was too much.

Lizzie was at a private nursery – just a little one, but exceptionally good. Then she got a place in the school nursery. She would have lunch at the private nursery, and at quarter past one they would take her to school. Then we picked her up at school. They were brilliant – and great for Lizzie: she knew exactly what was going on. Then in the September she started school full-time. Then Heather met another bloke, called Luke, and he was also an addict. It seems to me that wherever she went, she picked them up. People see that you're doing drugs; they'll latch onto the fact that you've got something – she had a flat. I think during the whole of this time she had, like, three flats.

And then she disappeared. And she's an adult, you know, we can't do anything about it – she chooses not to come. She was gone for about…10 weeks. During that time I was in pieces. Eventually I rang Bridge and said, 'My daughter is a drug addict, and I think she might be engaging with you. She's missing and we haven't seen her for so many weeks.'

I broke down. I said, 'I don't want to know if she's coming there, but please, if she is, can somebody ask her to get in touch with us, just to let us know that she's alive?' About an hour after, I got a phone call from Mary at Bridge. She said she couldn't say anything about whether Heather was going there or not, but in all this that was going on, who was looking after me? And...I just broke down again. I just said, 'Nobody'. But I had been going to the doctor's – I had counselling, because by this time I'd had to give up work.

I'd been off sick for three times, and eventually, the last time, management were just not sympathetic at all. It was a case of 'You can take extended leave without pay.' They have to give you your job back at the end of it, up to 5 years. But one of the management said to me, 'Well we can't keep carrying on, sick pay to *you*, and paying somebody else to do the job you're supposed to be doing.' He made me feel so *bad* about it that I came out of that meeting in tears, and, when I came home, I immediately rang Personnel and said that I wanted to hand me notice in. The woman in Personnel said, 'You are entitled to another 6 months on half-pay.' I said, 'I can't do it.' They'd made me feel so bad. She just said, 'Think about it – discuss it with your husband.' I just said, 'I just don't want it.' I was absolutely heartbroken – because I'd been so proud – I'd done this job for 26 years and gone from one department to another, and nobody had a bad word against me. Anyway, that was it – I had to give up work. And at this point Martin – we had his pension, and by now, he'd got a part-time job at the Tax Office.

Whilst Heather was missing, Martin and I began to see Mary. The two of us didn't use to discuss Heather, because I felt he was always very sympathetic towards her – and I was angry, *very* angry. So we went to Mary and we engaged with Mary and said how we felt to Mary, but we couldn't say those things to each other. I would break down. I was frightened for Heather. I was also afraid to say things to my family, because I felt so ashamed and such a failure – that I'd let her down somewhere, somewhere along the line, and also let down my family. I'm the youngest and my siblings are not in the best of health, and I didn't want them worrying about me. But it was obvious that they were worrying. Eventually, when I did tell them, it was a case of – 'Do you really think that we didn't know? That she was taking – we knew there was something.' But at some point afterwards one of them said to me, 'Just let Heather get on with it. Let her take Lizzie, she's all right now. You've got a life of your own.' I said, 'I can't do that. I can't do it.' Heather wasn't all right.

She were missing for 10 weeks before she got in touch with us, then she sent us an email, saying she'd like to meet us. It was nearly Christmas. We arranged to meet her in a café. And I walked past her – I didn't recognise her! She was so thin, gaunt – dirty – and obviously hungry. She just said, 'Mum', and I turned round, and how I didn't faint on the spot...anyway I just gave her a hug, like you would – it's your child, isn't it? I were just so relieved to see her alive. I said, 'Come on, we'll go and get something sweet.' We sat there for an hour. We couldn't question her much. Just, 'Are you all right? Where're you living?' 'Oh, I'm living with somebody' – a flat in Bosley I think it was – 'His name's Luke.' 'Are you still using?' 'I'm trying not to.' It was pretty obvious she still was. It was so dreadful. 'But I want you to know I'm all right', she said. She asked if we could bring Lizzie, and said she'd got something for her for Christmas.

So we met again before Christmas, with Lizzie, who was about 6 now. I took some Christmas things. Not expensive things that she could sell for drug money. Things like warm clothes, boxes of chocolates, smellies, deodorant. Lizzie was all right with her, but a bit distant. Heather gave her something that had obviously come from the pound shop, or she'd been given. I said, 'Heather... Can't you do something about this? Can't you do something about it?' And she broke down and told me she was pregnant to Luke, and I said, 'What are you going to do?' 'I'm having it.'

A Turning Point?

I can't remember now how it came about, but she engaged again with Bridge. She was on methadone now. They managed to organise for her to go to a kind of rehab place in Oldham whilst she was pregnant. That was the turning point. We went to see her with Lizzie every weekend and she was allowed to come home a couple of times. And she came to us – and not to Luke. But he was still on the scene. When she went into labour she was still in Oldham. I got the phone call to say she was in labour, and could we pick Luke up? I said, 'No, we can't.' Martin and I went to Oldham, but of course, by the time we got there, he was already there. He'd got in anyway. Frances was born about five to midnight. She wasn't taken to special care, although Heather told us she had lapsed and taken drugs twice whilst she were there. Now it was a case of, 'When I come out, can I come to your house?'

Luke wasn't around very often. He appeared occasionally. I think that Heather might even have gone to his parents at some point, but eventually she appeared at our house with Frances. It was pretty obvious that his parents didn't want anything to do with this baby. I remember then, after that, her being at our bungalow with Frances. But I had mixed feelings. You're angry! As much as you love them, you're *sad* and grieving. It's like a bereavement, because you've *lost* that child that you knew, and they've become somebody else, totally different, somebody that's horrible, you know...

Anyway, to our surprise, at this point she seemed to change. She was still engaging with Bridge and doing quite well, and still only on methadone. She even managed, during that lucid period, and whilst Frances was little and at nursery, to do one year of a psychology degree here in Bradford! So this is what I mean about her being intelligent. But there's always the fear that she'll go down again, because you've seen it so many times.

There wasn't much room in the bungalow and eventually she moved out with Frances and ended up in another flat. Martin and I went in and decorated and got sorted out for her. But then suddenly, 'Oh, me boiler's been pinched.' I said, 'What do you mean, your boiler's been taken?' 'Oh, someone's broken in and...' 'How d'ye mean, broken in?' She said, 'I'll have to get in touch with t'council.' I thought it was suspicious. I'd go in, and it'd be untidy. Later she was living with Frances in another flat which was damp and horrible and riddled with mice. She would stay there at night, but come to us in the day, so she didn't actually spend a right lot of time there. She was definitely trying to get off drugs by this time. But sometimes she'd come and she'd sit here and she'd fall fast asleep, and I'd wonder if she was just tired. *I* couldn't tell.

I'd be looking after Frances, the children'd be at school and we'd walk down together to pick Lizzie up from school, so that Lizzie got used to seeing her mum come for her at school as well. But the two girls did not get on well. Lizzie's never got on with Frances. Never. She has no time for her – she still has no time for her. It's jealousy. 'Mum had that baby – and that baby stayed with my mum. My mum looked after *her*, but she didn't want *me*.' What we'd say to Lizzie was, 'She *did* want you. She was incapable of looking after you, so we looked after you until she *was* capable of looking after you.' As she's got older, and Lizzie now knows everything, she understands. But it does not help the relationship between her and Frances. She still has no time for Frances. She won't sit and listen to Frances read.

Heather was still with Bridge and she had a good key worker. She'd got a house on an estate now – yet another that we carpeted and gave her furniture for. She stayed there about a year until she got a swap for a slightly smaller house on Summerfield Road. Luke had disappeared off the face of the earth, I don't know why. She hadn't been with anybody else. And she'd been having these contraceptive injections. She'd been on her own, and she was doing okay, except for not continuing with her degree. In fact her uncle'd asked her if she wanted to do some gardening for him. He's her godfather; he knows everything. He did lots of corporate gardening – housing associations and things like that – and he needed someone to take on the little local gardens. So she did that for him and she got a little bit of money, on top of her benefits.

A Relapse

But then, when Frances was about 2, she met Wayne. Don't know where she met him, but lo and behold, when she moved into a new place, a few weeks after, Wayne moved in with her. Apparently he had been on the go for a while and coming and staying, and we didn't realise anything. Wayne seemed to be perfectly charming [at first]. He was also believed to do a bit of DIY and – you know – get stuck in, *but* whenever we went to the house, Frances was never downstairs. She was always upstairs. She wouldn't come downstairs until I'd say, 'What y'doing up there?'

By this time Frances'd probably be 3. Heather and Wayne were together for 2½, perhaps 3 years. She had another baby,

Peter, who was Wayne's child. He was absolutely his double to look at, which is horrible, cos he's such a horrible man. An' that's awful – don't get me wrong – Peter's such a lovely little boy. When Peter was due, Wayne rang us – 'She's in labour, you need to get here.' Later we found out that he'd pushed Heather down the stairs that morning. She was bruised all over. She had a hard time with the birth and she was in such pain.

They were at that house over a year. During that time she had numerous black eyes. One time I went and her eye was completely red. And I said, 'What have you done to your eye?' 'Oh, er, the baby put his thumb in it.' The door got broken. Then another time it was my brother-in-law's birthday, and we were all having a barbecue – it was summer. Wayne disappeared. When he came back it were obvious he'd been using – an' he and Heather had an argument. He insisted on setting off home with his baby, Peter. Heather followed. We got a taxi, just after – with Frances and Lizzie. At their house, Martin got out of the taxi and called the police because Wayne and Heather were arguing so violently that he was scared for them and for Frances. It turned out that the police had been called numerous times to that address because of domestic violence. This time Wayne was arrested.

Another night Wayne nearly strangled Heather and then kept her in the bedroom and wouldn't let her out, though both of the kids were with her in the room. Whilst he was asleep the following morning she got up, found the door open and took the kids to their other grandma's (Martin's mother). She were probably 81 or 82, at the time. Heather were bruised all over, she'd got marks that she tried to hide with a scarf. When we came home from wherever we were, we went straight to Martin's mum and found Heather there, sobbing. We said, 'When're you gonna throw him out? It's your house, not his.' 'Oh, he'll come back', she said, 'he'll come back.' Anyway, when we went back to the house he'd gone – along with the television, the children's electronic toys – anything that was of any value. But yet – she took him back! About three times she took him back, and he did it every time!

I was terrified. I was scared that he would physically harm her or the children – he'd just lash out – and he was a big 6 foot 3. As for the children, I think Frances liked him when he was being kind. And when we were there, we only ever saw that side of him. She were climbing trees at 3 years old. If anybody was there, he'd say, 'Come on Frances and play – we've got her a trampoline, we've got her this little Wendy house' – everything seemed to be fine. But I think, as soon as we'd gone, Frances was banished upstairs again, or sent out to play.

Out of all of Heather's children, I feel most sorry for Frances, cos she's the one that's had the hardest deal. Lizzie might think *she* has, but Frances is the one that's seen it all, experienced it all. Heather told me one night that Frances had wet the bed – she'd be about 3, and he pulled her out of the bed, pulled the carpet up from the floor and made her sit on the floorboards. Said she didn't deserve a bed. She saw him hitting her mother – definitely witnessed that. She used to hide under the trampoline sometimes. I thought she was playing hide and seek, but in hindsight I think she was hiding from *him*. She'd come and cling to me and say, 'Granny, can I sit on your knee?' Peter was too young to understand.

When Peter was just over a year old we discovered that Wayne had attacked Heather again. And he'd obviously done it in the interim too, because the police had been called and he'd served 2 months in prison for violence against her. But she still took him back! He wrote letters to us and told us it was all a load of lies – 'It's Heather, I really love her, she's paranoid, she's a schizophrenic, she's…' I opened the first letter like an idiot and read it, and was horrified. Every other letter, Martin just tore it up – didn't even open it. But eventually Wayne began to be so violent that she said, 'I have to get away – I have to get away from him completely – to break the habit of him coming back.' And by this time she was on Subutex [buprenorphine], a drug which makes users of heroin feel ill.

Moving On

My middle daughter's husband had just set up his own business and he generously offered Heather a job! So she moved to Lincolnshire, with Frances and Peter, into rented accommodation. I think she gave her notice on the house when Wayne was out or in prison, and before he came back she'd gone. Lizzie saw her sister and brother go off with their mother, and she wasn't going. But now with the Subutex, Heather was technically clean, so I asked Lizzie, 'Do you want to go with your mum this time?' And she said, 'No. I want to stay here, cos I don't want to leave all me friends.' I was relieved, though I think it made Lizzie realise that, 'Hang on, if she can look after them, why couldn't she look after me?'

During that period we were going down to Lincolnshire twice a month, or they came up here at weekends. They were in Lincolnshire for just over a year. Kay and her husband gave Heather such a lot of support. He employed her. He tried to sort out some of the mess that she'd got into with her debts. Got some of the smaller ones consolidated. They also got her a solicitor, because – can you believe it? – Wayne decided to take her to court for access to Frances and Peter! So then we had this court case going on as well. Out of her salary, she had to pay £200 a month to the solicitor, her rent, before-school club and after-school club for Frances, and Peter's nursery. So she had *nothing*. She had about £25 left. It took 2 years for the case to come to court, and at the first hearing, Wayne did not turn up. He was told he could not apply again for 4 years and then only under certain conditions like going on an anger management course.

Anyway, after a year, Heather said Frances was missing us so much that she would come back to Bradford. I must admit to being in two minds about it, because whilst she was there – I got to be honest – life was a bit more peaceful. All that time she was there, she was getting the Subutex for her treatment from Bridge. They agreed that they would carry on treating her, providing she came back every so often and had the tests, which she did. We were worn out with all this travelling though. Anyway, when she came back, she'd never removed her name off the housing list, and it just so happened that they were advertising two houses, about a mile away from us, so she put bids on two of them. She was very lucky to be offered one, where she's been now for over 2 years. But of course that's been another house which has all had to be carpeted, though we didn't mind this time.

It couldn't have been any better, but we couldn't at first get Frances back into the school that she'd left. Frances has had so many schools – six schools and she's only 8! But the biggest thing that happened since Heather came back is that Lizzie moved back with her. Everything happened at once at that time. About a month before Heather came back, I lost my twin brother, and there was his funeral. But, you know, I was so busy with sorting out Heather's new house, buying a cooker and a suite and things, that I didn't really have time to grieve for him.

And then Lizzie told me that she wanted to go live with her mum, because her mum was round the corner now and she could get to school from her mum's. And it were just like a double whammy. I'd lost me brother, now it was Lizzie.

She was 13, and from 2–13, I'd done everything. But Lizzie said, 'You always said that when me mum was well...' She'd obviously asked her mum, discussed it with her mum. I just said to Martin, 'Well we could say no', because we still had the Residence Order. But I'd always said to Lizzie, 'When your mum is well enough to look after you...' I couldn't go back on my word, and I had to trust Heather. But Heather and Lizzie have no idea how heartbroken I was. I have put a face on every day. It's harder still cos Lizzie is not at all demonstrative to anyone. I sometimes think she only ever gives me her love or anything if it's Christmas, or her birthday. I put my arms round her last night and she shrugged me off. It's as if I've always been the big bad wolf. She's forgotten about all the years when she used to climb into bed with me and we'd read stories. She once wrote me a note that said, 'I love you Grandma.' I had it in my purse, because that was so rare for Lizzie. Mostly it was, 'I want my mummy to notice me, and you're just Grandma.'

We had to let her go. For the first couple of weeks, she probably came back a couple of times and she'd say, 'Oh, I'm going to stay here tonight.' But then that was it. It was difficult at first for Heather, cos now she was coping with an older child. But Heather treats Lizzie like an adult. They're like sisters. Then occasionally she'll try to be, you know, a mum, trying to lay some ground rules. And of course it doesn't work, because 99 per cent of the time, they're... buddies. I said to Lizzie yesterday, 'What happened about your English test?' Cos she's A* quality, is Lizzie. But she got a C. I said, 'Why did you get a C?' 'I don't know. I'm going to re-sit it.' So she re-sat this test and got a B. I said, 'Why did you get a B?' She was angry: 'I don't know! Anyway what's wrong with a B?' I said, 'Two months ago you were A*. How come you've slipped to a B? Get your act together, because you shouldn't be complacent.' But it's me that's doing it, not her mother! If she were here, there'd be no phone and no telly until her homework were done. At Heather's, she goes to her bedroom, and she's on the phone all the time, television's on. She said, 'I do the homework, don't I?' Heather's only now trying to set some ground rules.

Reflecting on the Past

We've only ever permanently had Lizzie, but the others have spent so much time here, we might as well have brought them up too – it feels like they've always been here. You see them and you're so relieved that they've not been taken away and put into care. You see them grow and develop and you get that unconditional love. There was peace in my heart knowing that Lizzie hadn't gone into care, that we would never see her again. And it would have happened because Heather was obviously neglecting her. I would never have forgiven myself if anything had happened to Lizzie.

But sometimes, in and amongst it all, you do resent what you've given up – the lifestyle that you've had instead. It made me become a recluse – I didn't want to go anywhere, because I didn't want to talk about Heather. You've given up your life. One person said to me, 'What are you going to do? She could carry on having a baby every year – are you going to tek 'em all?' Without all this my life would have been very different – we'd just got to the point where financially we were finding things a bit easier, my job would have carried on and I'd have been able to retire with a full pension.

But the good news is that Heather's been clean now for 3 years. She's on nothing at all, not even methadone. It's like finding the child that you lost. She's got no memory of those years, of the horrid things. Whether she doesn't choose to think about it... She's trying to make up for it now. One of my sisters is getting a bit forgetful and Heather said, 'It'll be me that looks after you, Mum. Come and live with me, Mum, when you start getting like Auntie Sue.' At one point, my eldest daughter's husband wouldn't have her in the house. But then she started cleaning for them every week. She's gone from strength to strength and is now working full-time and studying. Lizzie has settled with her and there is no problem with Peter – though his father might reappear when he is 7 and allowed to apply to the court. He's just 5 now and we still have peace of mind. Only Frances still has major issues.

My family all felt for us, though with the drugs they sometimes found it difficult with Heather. My older sister has always been there for me. She welcomed Heather into her house, even when she knew she was using. She wouldn't give her money, but she'd give her food, or she'd say, 'Oh, I've got a jumper upstairs that's too big for me, or too small for me, or...' – you know what I mean. But even *she's* not always been able to understand where I'm coming from. Her boys have sailed through school, sailed through everything. All got professional jobs, all married... They've never put a foot wrong. She's never had to deal with being called into school, or, you know, it makes you feel envious!

I've had good friends too – two very good friends, that I worked with. They didn't know about the drugs, until I had to give up work – I told them at the end that it was drugs. They were horrified, but they were supportive for me. I was also exceptionally good friends with my neighbour next door, but she died suddenly, a few months after my brother. I was absolutely bereft at this stage. She had become such a special friend to me. I mean, I lost my brother, and I lost Lizzie and I lost my friend.

After we talked to Mary, Martin got so much more involved, and it was easier for us to speak about our fears to each other. Now he has a better job, employed by local government, though it's only on a yearly contract. We're both 60, so still we've got a lot of our life left. And the thing is, Heather is now doing so well, I feel confident that she'll never go back to that life. I said to her, 'Would you use again?' She said, 'Mum, I've got too much to lose. I've got Lizzie back. I've got Frances, I've got Peter. I've got my own home. I can do what I want.' She's trying to get back into work. She's just done this Level 2 Health and Social Care NVQ – she's even looking at going back to university. Although I'm confident that Heather will go on and do good things, *that fear* is still there – she'll meet somebody else and he'll be another user. It's happened four times. Of course she's saying to me, 'I'm not interested in men, I'm happy on my own', and I think, 'Well, good', but – she's young. She's only 32. Half of her life has gone – she's 32 and she's got a 15-year-old!

I think Martin is too soft with Heather. She only has to ask and he's there. She's now taking responsibility for maintaining her own house, which is something. She started to decorate so she painted the walls but she didn't finish off, and Martin said, 'Oh I'm going to our Heather's just to finish that bit for her.' And he pays for the mobile phone, he organised a car for her, that's in his name, and she pays him and he pays the finance. If he didn't do it, she wouldn't be able to afford it. We pay for all Lizzie's out-of-school activities – still do – all her dancing, all her costumes, all her shoes...

Of course we have to help – she still has debts. This is what comes up to haunt them afterwards even when they're doing well – the past catches up with them. As the parent, you're fearful that that past might kick them back into the abyss. If they're still using they don't worry about it, whereas if they're not, then they've got to think about the consequences.

And of course the children have suffered. Frances is 9 now and she sometimes talks about Wayne: 'I don't like Wayne, because he's a bad man. He won't come back, will he?' Frances has so many issues – behavioural issues – and no wonder. She slams doors, shouts that she hates everybody, runs upstairs. She bullies Peter, but she can't see that what she's doing to Peter is exactly the same as what Lizzie did to her. By bullying, I mean she'll tease him, take his toys off him. But mostly she's quite good with him. But she's wetting the bed still. Every night. And she won't go upstairs on her own. She just switches, does Frances sometimes. She can be as good as gold, and then she just goes, like that. Won't get up off the floor – you've got to get down and pull her. She won't get herself ready, won't do her work. It's very hard to live with. But then she can be fantastic. We had a family party on Saturday, and Frances did pass-the-parcel with all the little ones – set the music, and picked all the rubbish up afterwards. She was brilliant.

It's hard, as a grandparent. Frances's with her mum, and yet she knows that I'm a soft pushover. When she gets in trouble with her mum, I find myself sticking up for her. When really, I ought to keep my distance and say, 'No, if your mummy said this, that's it.' But I feel so sorry for this poor child, in the middle. She's such a loving child as well – all she wants sometimes is a little bit of attention.

And Lizzie, who's 16 now – don't forget her mother had said to her: '*They* don't want you. They just don't want *me* to have you.' Maybe that stuck with her. You know – 'They don't want me mum to have me.' Sometimes Lizzie's behaviour was very erratic. She had a lot of anger in her. We got in touch with CAMHS [Child and Adolescent Mental Health Services]. Someone there saw her and tried to engage with Heather and Wayne, but Wayne wouldn't go. I think it helped Lizzie. But she only went a couple of times, and that was it, then she was fine. She's always had this jealousy though – I fear she has no feeling at all for Frances.

Of course Lizzie's dad, Matt, is lovely, and he's still around! She sees him every fortnight. He's offered to pay £75 towards her French exchange trip, but he doesn't pay maintenance now. His second partner had two children – and then they split up, and apparently he does pay maintenance to them. But, as I say, he's been there all Lizzie's life. He's been a part of her life. And he's not a drug user. He's never been involved in it.

Frances has had the worst deal. Peter escaped it, because when he was 1, they moved to Lincolnshire. He doesn't remember Wayne. He doesn't know who his dad is. He only ever relates to Martin, and his uncle. He absolutely adores Martin – he's his father figure. He wouldn't put his shoes on this morning, and all I have to say to Peter is, 'Do I have to tell Grandad you've been a naughty boy?' 'I'll do it now!' he says.

The Grandparents Group

We joined The Grandparents Group when it first started in 2005. Mary said that she had several grandparents, who were all seeing her for the same reason, and she thought that it might be a good idea if we got together, to compare notes, or maybe we could help each other out in a different way. And that's what happened.

Me and Martin seem to be the only ones in the group where our children have successfully abandoned drugs. I sometimes feel guilty for still coming to the group – I suspect everybody else feels a bit envious – I would feel that if it was me! But I get *so* much comfort still from that group, because that's the place that I can say, 'Well this is what happened and it does still hurt, and this is what I fear.' I suspect the fears will never completely disappear.

* * *

Editorial Commentary

As parents, most of us have done our best to divert our children from drug and alcohol addiction, but given the lack of knowledge and support, we feel ourselves to have failed. This story is our only example of a successful outcome, though the parents continue to fear a relapse. This underlines what we learnt at Bridge – that escaping addiction takes many years and will only work when substance users are helped to empower *themselves*.

However, we see again the failure by state agencies to take seriously the concerns of grandparents that their grandchildren are unsafe. It is not only that the law sides with those who have parental rights; it is also an assumption that drug addicts can perform adequately as parents, and a wilful disregard or ignorance of the damage being inflicted on children in the process.

Lack of meaningful intervention (although health visitors and schools receive favourable mentions) may lead grandparents into dangerous confrontations with their adult children and partners. More often they must look on in fear and dismay as the situation deteriorates. Initially here the grandparents were only able to offer a safe house on a revolving-door basis, although they eventually persuaded their daughter to agree to a Residence Order to secure the oldest grandchild's care. When Heather returned to live in the family home, she brought with her the drugs and the addictive behaviour, compromising the safety of her child. A second unplanned pregnancy led to a period of rehab organised by Bridge. This began to strengthen her capacity to resist, but the situation now entailed not only escaping addiction, but also escaping the brutality of partners and the chaos of lives marked by debt and insecurity. We see how drug use deadens an addict's capacity to face consequences – a particular example is indebtedness; another is the impact of stealing to fund the habit, with its inevitable consequences of loss of trust within the family. Another child was born and there was more grief before Heather was finally successful.

Again, we can identify how a successful drug agency was able to go the extra mile, facilitating conversation between Emma and Martin about what was tearing them apart, and going beyond the drug user to show concern for those who live the nightmare of caring for them and their children. Emma is insightful about the particular damage done to the middle child, who has experienced the worst neglect and insecurity and is now acting out her distress.

We do not know enough about the healing that is possible once a parent relinquishes their addiction or about the longer-term effects of drug use on development. It is clear, however, that the grandparents' support is still needed.

6

Mischa

'No regrets'

Mischa's grandson, Nile, was taken into care owing to her daughter's heavy drug use, and she then fought for 5 months to get him back. At the time of this interview he was 7 and she was a single parent of 75.

* * *

My story begins with a terrible loss. It was 9pm on a Friday evening, 7 years ago, when the doorbell rang. Two grim-faced police officers and one social worker stood there. They said that they had come to take my grandchild into care due to the behaviour of my daughter Anya. Despite my desperate pleas and my daughter offering to leave so that he could stay with me, they left with him shortly afterwards – a tiny baby, less than 2 months old, fast asleep. I have never been so distressed in my life, except perhaps when my mother died. I could not stop weeping, with my son and daughter trying vainly to comfort me. My daughter was upset too, but seemed to accept what had happened – it was a fate suffered by many of her friends – almost normal.

My daughter is a substance abuser – heroin and cocaine – and had been an addict since her mid-teens. She is adopted and had suffered the kind of neglectful and violent start in life which no child should endure. When I adopted her she was already 5 and quite damaged by her early experiences. She had devised strategies to survive that were counter-productive in a normal family, and she stretched me to the limits, with challenging and controlling behaviour which eventually led in her teenage years to putting herself at risk of involvement with drugs and drug dealers. Despite all my efforts I was unable to prevent her from sinking down into a sordid and dangerous life. She was groomed, abducted, beaten, often missing and still she went back to the perpetrators for more. I appealed to police and eventually to Social Services. No one helped – and Social Services blamed me for her situation, rather than offering some intervention to get her off the drugs. Even in her 30s, she was leading a chaotic life, without a permanent abode, resorting to prostitution to support her need for drugs.

It had been disturbing then to receive a text message from her saying that she was pregnant and wanted to keep the child (she had already suffered a couple of miscarriages). I met up with her at a project set up to support sex workers. She told them that if she were not allowed to keep the baby (she had a string of convictions for drug- and violence-related crimes, as did the man whom she claimed as the father of her child) she wanted me to bring it up. 'No way', I said, 'I'm 68 – how can I take on a baby?'

The (putative) father went into prison soon afterwards for 2½ months. My pregnant daughter was provided with a small flat and began to receive benefits. She seemed to settle down whilst he was away and I did my best to help with visits and buying equipment for the baby. But then he came out of prison, joined her in her flat and they sank back into the old life of drugs, violence and petty criminality. The maternity benefit went on drugs. Social Services were involved and there was at least one meeting, to which I was invited, but it was very unclear what was to happen when the baby was born – I think they said we'd wait and see. Despite disclosing her relapse back into hard drugs (the man did not turn up) no planning process was set up.

In the event, she fell out with the boyfriend and he locked her out of her own flat. She then went to stay with friends living the same life as her. The baby, Nile, was born a month prematurely, after an evening of drug taking. Suddenly the Social Services swung into action and announced that they had applied for a Protection Order on the child and that my daughter could not take him from hospital unless I agreed to take them in. I didn't see I had a choice, though no prior planning or assessment of my circumstances had taken place. Social workers visited me at home that day and stayed about three-quarters of an hour, briefly reviewing my experience, but there was no form filling. I asked them to look round the house – they did not insist on this or seem to be concerned. I was relieved the baby was safely born and, though tiny, he seemed to be healthy and normal. He was kept in the hospital for 2 weeks whilst they checked him out. To everyone's surprise he displayed no overt symptoms of drug withdrawal, but Anya was not allowed to breastfeed him, and for the first time I felt for her distress at this.

I was very uneasy to have my daughter back home with me – after more than a decade of fruitlessly trying to get her off drugs and coping with her behaviour, I did not trust her to behave reasonably. On the other hand, I thought that if she were ever going to change, this was the opportunity. So I rushed around, clearing a room in my house for them and getting all the stuff one needs for a small baby. I made it clear that the boyfriend was not to come to the house.

I assumed that I would have support if he turned up or she became violent and transgressed the rules we agreed for us to live together. And at first I was impressed. She wanted the baby and was very taken with him and eager to learn how to manage him. She got anxious if he cried and would come and ask me to calm him, but he was not a difficult baby at all. I got her into a college course to do basic English and maths, and I tried to encourage her into learning some cooking skills and going to mother-and-baby groups. We shared some of the child care, but I wanted her to bond with the baby and understand her responsibilities, so I tried to provide back-up rather than intervene. At this time we also had some support from Bridge, a drug rehabilitation project, though my daughter made little effort to get involved. This was a project which also helped family members to cope with their children's substance abuse and it organised The Grandparents Group.

About a month after Nile's birth I asked for help from Social Services (whom I had not seen since the birth) as I had to go away for 2 nights. My grown-up son was still living with me then and my daughter was full of promises (including to the social worker) that all would be well. Instead, she rang her boyfriend and he came over whilst my son was at work. When my son found them at home he was incensed – and then suddenly they were on the doorstep with the baby in his pram. My son chased the boyfriend away and my daughter called the police, only to tell them all was fine when they arrived. I was shocked at her disregard for the baby and her obsession with a man who at other times she was ready to abuse and dismiss. He had been involved in domestic violence both with his previous partner and my daughter (though she can be violent too). She had also broken the agreement that he was not to come to the house.

A month after this she sneaked out of the house with the baby and disappeared. When they didn't come back I was beside myself with fear and rang the police and Social Services. The police began looking for her and Social Services said there would be a meeting. There was some talk of the baby going to a foster parent and I said, 'Why, when I am here?' However, I thought the meeting would give me the chance to complain about our lack of support and to ask for advice to prevent my daughter from behaving in this dangerous way. I wanted to ask whether I had the right or the capacity to stop a grown woman from leaving the house. Late on the second day, my daughter came back of her own accord (the police were always one step behind her). Thankfully the baby seemed safe, but she was high on drugs and in an angry mood, abusing the police officer who came to check on her return.

The Social Services meeting was pre-empted by the removal of the baby the following day, a Friday. I knew what the impact of this trauma could be on such a small child – to wake up from his sleep amongst total strangers! He was moved to one foster parent and then removed again after 2 weeks to another. I thought he had survived the drugs and violence which accompanied the pregnancy, but now he was deliberately being traumatised by the state – and no one listened! I spent the weekend writing a statement of what had happened and finding a solicitor, as we had been told there would be a hearing on the Monday morning. In the event, I was excluded from full participation in the case – grandmothers apparently had no rights to be represented, despite me having taken in my daughter and grandchild. Indeed, it was clear that suspicion was also falling on me. It was implied that I had somehow colluded in her behaviour, or casually allowed her to go off with the baby. Not that anyone asked me for a statement about what had happened, but through the solicitor I was able to submit mine to the court, and at the judge's discretion I was allowed to sit in at the back. Meanwhile the putative father *was* included in proceedings without question – though at that point he was torn between denying that it was his child and insisting that he be consulted. Nile was put on a temporary Care Order.

The next few months were a nightmare. I had to get a separate solicitor from my daughter as our interests were now seen to be potentially in conflict, and whilst her (and the father's) legal fees were paid, I had to dig deep into my savings to the tune of some thousands to cover the extensive costs. There were endless court hearings and Social Services meetings, all of which I attended, to ensure that I was not excluded again. My daughter – and eventually I – were allowed contact with Nile, but at cheerless centres under social workers' surveillance. My daughter had more contact time than I was allowed. Meanwhile she was still living with me as she had nowhere else to go, but this was an ordeal for me. I couldn't forgive her for what she had done to lose her baby and I feared her volatility. It was all I could do to keep it together. Social Services began a process of assessing her to have the baby back, but just as they decided that this was too risky, my daughter created a scene at home, smashed things up and left. She went back to the man whose violence she often spoke of. I was relieved, but depressed and horrified that she would return to him. The two of them then brazenly put in a joint bid to have Nile placed with them, and to my astonishment Social Services began another process of assessment. The 'father' (but see later) was now also allowed contact time.

I was shaken at this turn of events – how could Social Services even think of returning a vulnerable child to such people, with a history of drugs and violence? I decided to apply to foster Nile myself and a second process of assessment was begun with me (at last). By now I was 69, and although I had a blameless record, was in fairly good health and had considerable experience of caring for children – I had adopted children who were now grown up – there was scepticism from the social worker to whom I was assigned that I would get through the panel. He would say, 'You would be perfect, if it wasn't for your age.' Many gruelling hours – well at least 15! – of interviews took place before they were satisfied. At the same time, Anya and her boyfriend were being assessed, and we now saw Nile separately. I found the artificial setting of the centre uncomfortable and at times humiliating, as staff had to follow you to the toilet with the child and would give out advice that seemed inappropriate when I had already brought up children. But they were well-meaning and only doing their job. I did not feel as if I was getting closer to Nile during these sessions, although he was smiley and loved to play. The foster mother also impressed me by her kindness and care for him.

Court hearings to renew the Care Order went on, and the judge eventually ordered a DNA test on the putative father. It came back negative! What a relief to know that Nile did not carry the genes of this man, whom then I would have had to deal with in some way or another, if only to tell Nile who he was. At the same time it left Nile without a named father – history repeating itself, as my adoptive daughter's father was also unknown. Eventually, after more incidents of domestic violence between Anya and this man, their bid to have Nile was turned down.

At last I was put forward to go to the foster care panel – by now with the social worker's support. To my relief, and some amazement, I got through the panel. I now became a 'friends and family' foster carer. I was asked at the panel if I was aware that children whose mothers had used drugs during pregnancy had a higher-than-normal chance of suffering ADHD. I am pretty familiar with the literature on adoption and the challenges that children enduring the loss of parents can bring – including labels such as ADHD and others – so I said I was aware, and just hoped it would not happen – after all, had Nile not seemed to recover from his premature birth without the anticipated withdrawal symptoms?

Now I was on a stipend – not a large amount of money, but helpful nevertheless. At the same time I was a servant of Social Services and expected to abide by their rules. I could never be certain of Nile's long-term security under these terms. I was too old in law to adopt him, so again I returned to court to apply for a Special Guardianship Order, which would give me most parental rights, and him almost as much security as if he were adopted. This took another year, but was eventually granted, and following this I received a financial award which tapered off after a couple of years.

Nile Comes Home

Meanwhile Nile came home at last, after 5½ months away in foster care. Superficially he settled in well, but having had adopted children I could sense his holding back on me for months before he finally claimed me as his own. I was so proud of him and he progressed well and met all the usual developmental milestones.

I thought it was important that Nile knew he had a mother and that she did not become a fantasy in his head, so during the court proceedings we set up some regular contact time – once every 2 months for a couple of hours. It had been suggested to me by the court guardian that letterbox contact would be enough, but Anya was my daughter and I still felt responsible for her and did not want to exclude her entirely. I set out with some trepidation on this path, hoping we could manage it. It was not easy – she had relapses and missed many contact meetings. When she did come she behaved well to Nile, very caring and pleased to see him. He treated her more or less like other friends of mine, but it is clearly important to him to know he has a 'mum', like other children. More recently I have begun to tell him, in words that he can understand, why he doesn't live with her. Like most children at this age he takes this as just a factual account, and does not seem distressed. Probably later he will want to know more. As for the absent father, Nile has worked this out for himself – 'I call him zero dad', he announced recently. I thought this was fair and accurate.

I can't pretend that it was easy to take on a small child. Muscles that had weakened cranked painfully back into use as I struggled with buckles and poppers and pushchairs. At the end of each day I was exhausted. But somehow I also rose to the challenge. It was exhilarating and a wonderful new lease of life to be caring for a little child and thinking of their future, working out routines that would allow us to manage it together and planning expeditions and holidays. However, although I was retired I was still working on projects and writing and I didn't want to abandon this work, which was important to my life and sense of self. I also needed some recovery time from the active physical toil of child care. What I found very difficult whilst I was fostering Nile was a stipulation that any babysitters or childminders had to go through extensive police checks. I just wanted occasional help to go out in an evening to a meeting or to see friends, but few were willing to babysit under these terms. And after the first few months I yearned for some time to work and recover from the hard physical toil. I asked if Nile could go to a nursery part-time, and to my relief this was acceptable as the staff are already vetted.

At first he went for 2 half-days, gradually increasing to 3 full days a week when he was 2 and until he moved to primary school. The nursery was good and I felt secure that he was safe and happy there. I also started to make one or two friends who had young children – this seemed really important to me. I have a fantastic circle of close friends, many of long standing, but they were mostly near my age and indeed were scattered across the country and the world as our lives had unfolded in different directions. What's more, not all of them supported my decision to take on Nile – indeed most of them were appalled that I would even consider this; and one or two, with my best interests at heart, were angry that I would not be able to enjoy retirement after a life of hard work and many challenges. Whilst I also felt the sudden loss of my independence and freedom, I could not have enjoyed life knowing that my grandchild was in care, probably going from one foster home to another, maybe in the end being adopted and lost to me forever. I did not regret what I had done, despite its difficulties. In the end nearly all my friends came round to accept my decision and went on caring about me.

After Nile started to go to nursery I felt rested and less pressured and our time together also blossomed. We began to go on weekly trips, nearly always on buses or trains. Nile loved anything with wheels! Now my age was in my favour as I had a free bus pass and a senior rail card, and Nile did not have to pay until he was 5, so we could freely roam the countryside. I looked out for free places to visit – museums, parks, woods and seasides, where we had great picnics and Nile was alert and curious and good company. He slept well and ate well and was beginning to chatter and entertain himself and me. We had fun together.

Eventually Nile became the usual 'terrible 2-year-old', demanding and noisy and into everything. When this behaviour continued into his third and fourth year I began to be concerned. I observed a couple of tantrums getting out of hand at nursery and was increasingly under pressure at home as he resisted normal controls and was frequently restless and hyperactive. He had little sense of his own safety and would disappear if I didn't hold onto him. His unruly behaviour was sometimes noticed by others, who would say, 'He's a handful, isn't he?' or 'My, he's got lots of energy!' I didn't feel that I was handling it very successfully and, whilst my other children had also been challenging, this was different and bewildering. My reading had alerted me to think that the drugs my daughter took during pregnancy had led to some neurological impairment and that the traumatic events of his first few months had made this worse. I asked for help and got an appointment with a paediatrician and psychologist, but no one seemed certain, and friends and family tended to dismiss my concerns – he was a boy, they said, all children have these phases. Nor did his nursery make any issue out of his behaviour. And when he reached the transition to 'big school' I took it for granted that he would settle in fine, even though (as it happened) he had to move to a school where he knew no one. I was totally unprepared for the events of the following 2 weeks as the head called me in with news that Nile was unmanageable, creating a lot of disruption, refusing to do as asked and, being unable to keep still, was hurting other children.

It was sheer luck that I chose this particular school. Once they got over the initial shock they responded magnificently, brought in several professionals and attended to the issues without regard to the cost. A wonderful behavioural team, who move from school to school, set up a programme for Nile, which involved a high level of support and positive feedback as well as genuine caring and love for him. They trained all the other staff who dealt with him and kept him out of serious trouble, and also ensured that he had the same opportunities for learning that other children have. He had relapses and bad days, but he began to be able to sit with others on the carpet to listen to stories and to work better with other children. And he was making progress with reading and maths and contributing to class discussion. What is more, they kept me in the process, sharing the issues and decisions. I was made to feel like a vital part of Nile's progress and praised for doing a fantastic job. Whilst I hardly felt I deserved this – indeed the turn of events had led to quite a major period of depression and sense that I had failed, first with Nile's mother and then with him – it was in striking contrast to my earlier experiences when my daughter went off the rails and I was endlessly blamed by social workers.

When Nile was 7, the behavioural team were able to withdraw except for a watching brief, and after the first year, the school applied for a Statement (now called an Education, Health and Care Plan). Now the school is resourced to service his needs, whereas before they were funding this out of normal resources. He has a wonderful worker, who keeps him safe and ensures that his behaviour does not lead him into trouble. There is so much positive feedback and he is doing well and more or less keeping up with other children academically. They have also organised for him to be seen by workers at the Child and Adolescent Mental Health Service [CAMHS], though this has not been very productive to date.

Thinking About the Future

I had hoped that taking Nile on so early would avoid some of the problems that my adopted children faced, but I have had to accept what fate has delivered. I can see that he is going to struggle to fulfil his potential in life and to cope with any changes, and I can only hope that we continue to be supported (the Statement does commit to resources for him until he is 25 if he stays in education or training). And of course, even whilst my whole conception of the future has been transformed by having a child to care for – and transformed for the better – I cannot help but worry in case I cannot see him through to adulthood. For a start I am on my own and my family, though supportive, does not live near enough to help me on a day-to-day basis. I do have my own house and a decent pension from work. I rarely get seriously ill, though when I had to have a hernia operation (a day case but with several days in bed afterwards) my eldest son came to help me and looked after Nile. Occasionally I have a day or so of illness and at first a neighbour, who is also a good friend, stepped in to care for Nile. Now she is usually at work but I have a few others whom I can also trust. All the same, when I had a serious bout of flu recently I had to manage alone and it was very hard. I am very lucky to have so many friends; it is just a pity most of them live so far away. However, this also means that we have managed a few lovely visits, touring around a few friends and not overstaying our welcome at any one place! People of my age often find young and exuberant children like Nile a strain. Actual holidays have sometimes been more of a problem, given Nile's hyperactivity, and I have lost at least one friend who did not understand that he was not simply 'spoilt' and 'naughty'. Until he was 4 I had to use the pushchair or reins all the time just to keep him safe. But then he gradually began to want to be near me, rather than to disappear, and life was a bit easier. I still need to hold his hand on the road though.

The hardest times with Nile are when he refuses to do what he is asked – won't come when he is called, won't sit still to eat, jumps up and down on a bus or races round the aisles and takes things off the shelf in the supermarket. He constantly meddles with things and raids cupboards.

Things happen around him – things go missing, there are unexplained breakages or damage and he is unable to own up. He is harder to control than my other children were and I have had to devise all sorts of ways to distract and encourage him. I am not as strong as I was, and I have less energy, and he tries my patience in ways that I thought I could never manage. But there are compensations. The happiest times with Nile are when I see him make strides in his understanding or ability – he is now an above-average reader as a result of my insisting on reading every night despite his wriggles and resistance. Just to hear him do this makes my heart swell with pride and joy. He is learning to swim and to dance, and though he doesn't always concentrate, he is making tremendous progress and enjoying the experience. His breaststroke is fantastic! And he's passed his Grade I [in swimming].

Our trips continue and it is exciting to set off for the day to places that I would not go to if I didn't have him – Scarborough with a heavy sea mist descending, the airport to try and see planes landing and instead looking at a tribute to lost airmen, Egyptian mummies at more than one local museum, adventure playgrounds galore, mysterious pictures in art galleries. It's not always easy to hold his attention, but he can be captivated and engaged. Occasionally we go to a classical music concert where children are welcome – so unusual! – and he is interested in the instruments and listens quietly to Vivaldi and Bach. He has been delighted by performances of *The Mikado* and *Nutcracker*, and it is a pleasure to see his smiles as he recognises music he knows from DVDs. Or I meet up with a younger friend with children at a play centre – we go to quite a few of these – so that the children can play safely and we can talk and enjoy a coffee. For now I am enjoying the responsibility and the loving excitement that comes with having a child who still wants a kiss and a cuddle and learns new things every day.

In The Grandparents Group we all worry about what will happen to our children when we are gone. Because we know what a huge sacrifice it is to take on a child, it is almost impossible to raise the subject with others who might step in. Certainly for me, it was too big a thing to ask of anyone, even though it would have been a relief to know that Niles' future was secured. And his emotional and behavioural issues make this even harder. But then a miracle occurred. My family have always stood by me, especially my sister and her husband. Her daughter (my niece), Ella, and her husband have long taken an interest in Nile and asked to take him on outings once a month, despite having a lively son a few months younger than Nile. Nile looks forward to these trips and it gives him a view of another kind of more normal family life. I couldn't bring myself to ask her directly, but my sister knew of my fears of leaving Nile if I died before he grew up. She passed these on to Ella and, one day, Ella let me know that if (when) anything happened to me, they could not see Nile go into care and would take him on. Of course I have laid down for her how hard this might be, not just because of his unpredictable behaviour, but also in terms of disrupting her own family (I can remember intensely how Anya's arrival turned our family upside down). I want her to know that she is not bound by her offer and must make a decision in the light of all the factors when I die or can't manage anymore. But they are great parents and have such good sense and intelligence that I am reassured that Nile will be cared for.

The Grandparents Group: Supporting Each Other

When Anya was still at home I met the organiser of The Grandparents Group and she encouraged me to come along for some support. I was reluctant at first – I seemed to be overwhelmed with problems that left me no time to think of myself. And I was uncertain what kind of people I would meet there. I have been in other support groups – particularly around adoption – but I wondered if in this case we would have anything in common beyond sharing the wrenching experience of having a child with drug addictions. But when I finally decided to give it a try I was immediately warmed by the way we shared our continuing grief over our children and our fears for the grandchildren we were now responsible for. Our situations are not ones which other people can generally understand or even sympathise with, so it was a relief to be able to talk openly about coping with it all. And we laughed as well as cried when we shared our happiness at our children's progress and resilience. In many ways taking on our grandchildren was similar to the adoption experience – these were traumatised children, displaying many of the symptoms that adopted children show, and we were struggling to make sense of it all. We still had our own children to live with as well, and this gave us an extra burden in many cases, though it also gave us some insight into why the grandchildren were behaving as they did – we knew their background intimately, unlike most adoptive parents. My impression is that we are good parents, bringing our knowledge of life and childraising to a new generation, though we often despair at not being able to manage it better. In general, this group was also struggling to get recognition and adequate material support – hearing of the hardships some were going through was heartbreaking. And the way that society was dealing with us was so depressingly inconsistent, often without understanding or appreciation of our efforts.

Where to Next?

I cannot think of giving up Nile now – I cannot imagine circumstances in which he would be better off with his mother, and I would fight all the way to keep him. Recently she has spent a year in prison after being caught stealing a large amount of money. She got clean in prison and looked healthier and, to be honest, she thrived in an institutional situation where you are (mostly) safe, if not free. With time on her hands she wrote to Nile nearly every week, although the letters displayed a romanticised version of her relationship with him – 'Your mum loves you so much' and 'I miss you so much.' I persuaded her that Nile should know where she was and why, and not be misled by the illusion of a bountiful, pure mother pining away. He took it in his stride, and did not appear to miss her. Once out, she went straight back to the man who has abused her, and she seems to have no plans for a different life. The letters stopped and she began missing the contact times again.

I expect Nile will be a trial in his adolescence, but I will deal with that as and when it arises. I can only do my best and hope I have the strength to continue whilst he needs me. He has opened a new world for me and I am grateful.

* * *

Editorial Commentary

Our stories have much in common, but there are distinctive features to each. In this case Social Services failed to protect Mischa's daughter and looked set to mishandle the protection of her grandchild. Then they overreacted, taking the child into emergency care without preparation or full assessment and without consideration of alternative courses of action.

This was at the time of the 'Baby P' media storm, when Haringey Children's Services were being severely criticised after the brutal murder of a 2-year-old by his mother, also incriminating her boyfriend and another man.

Mischa's daughter and grandchild were living with her under the terms of a Protection Order, yet she received no support or advice to prevent her daughter disappearing with the child. She had no right of representation at the court case that followed, eventually paying for legal representation, whilst her daughter and the child's putative father got legal aid. Despite them having a long history of drugs, violence and criminality, they were allowed to bid for restitution of the child to their care. Given that this was eventually refused, the child would have remained in care had Mischa not gone on fighting to have him back.

Caroline Archer explains that a child may suffer even before birth from a mother's long-term use of hard drugs and from the stressful and violent life she may be living [see Afterword]. Here, additional trauma was experienced owing to premature birth and neonatal separation of the child from the mother for recovery. Breastfeeding was not permitted. Although a period of calm followed and some bonding occurred, it soon shattered as the mother could not resist returning to her addiction of many years. A sudden and forcible severing of the baby's relationship with its mother and grandmother, and periods in two different foster homes, could not but mark Nile's development. After a period of funded foster care, Mischa decided to apply for a Special Guardianship Order to secure the child's future with her.

Signs of trauma may not be immediately obvious, though when Mischa applied to become a kinship carer, she was warned that her grandchild may develop ADHD. By the time the child was 3 or 4 years old, he was beginning to show a disturbing level of hyperactivity, impulsivity and resistance to ordinary parental controls. He was diagnosed with ADHD when he was 7 and after periods of aggression and lack of self-regulation. Medication is now helping him, as is the exceptional care at school, once the head had called in professional help with some wonderful collective strategies.

Contact arrangements are an issue for most grandparents. Mischa maintains a limited relationship with the child's mother, even when it involves telling the child some unpleasant truths. Mischa's adult daughter was herself a 'victim' of grooming and sexual predation as well as addiction, but Mischa feels she must now put the child first. Understandably she finds unconditional forgiveness difficult, following Anya's disappearance with Nile and her reckless behaviour leading to his reception into care.

Mischa's determination to stick with her grandchild despite – or because of – his difficulties is notable; and she has turned her life upside down to make a difference to his future, as well as planning in the event of her being unable to see him through to adulthood. What is remarkable is the lack of regret, and as with our other grandparents, the joy in her grandchild's progress and the loving bond she has with him.

7

Shelly

'They make you feel like it's your fault'

Shelly and her husband Brian found themselves, in their late 50s, taking on their daughter's three children, all of whom have disabilities. Their daughter, Caitlin, was unable to care for them after she became an alcoholic and was subject to domestic abuse. Caitlin died, leaving Lucas (now 11), Lee (7) and Joshua (5).

* * *

Social Services brought our grandsons, Lucas and Lee, to our house in 2008. They knocked on the door and brought them from their house, after a drunken fight between my daughter and her violent partner. Lucas was 4 and Lee was 5 months old. The social workers said they removed the boys from my daughter, Caitlin, due to emotional neglect. We explained we were not in the best position to manage, as we were both working full-time and we were not financially well-off enough to quit our jobs. We were assured that the arrangement would only be for a short time.

Caitlin's problems actually go way back – she went off the rails at the age of 14. She is the youngest of three, with an older brother and sister. Me and my husband both worked full-time as they were growing up, and the children never needed a minder. I worked any job that could fit around them, usually unsocial hours (nights) and my husband worked the day shift. Thinking back, maybe I was not always there for them, but we needed the money like most families did, to ensure they had nice things and at least be able to go on holiday once a year. My children had a lovely life growing up. Caitlin was a beautiful, gentle, little girl who was so clever and always polite. She was the academic one of the family: reading at the age of 4 and getting really good reports from school. While they were growing up, we took plenty of video footage of holidays and all those other special occasions. When she was younger, we were very close: she wouldn't go to bed without my t-shirt for comfort.

But then, for no apparent reason, Caitlin began to drink heavily. She had arguments with everyone within the family and became unnecessarily foul-mouthed. She stole money from us, to feed her alcoholic addiction. She was mixing with the wrong type of people quite close to where we lived, especially one older woman. This woman had children of her own and Caitlin befriended her daughter – they were about the same age. Caitlin used to visit this woman secretly. It was a long time before I became aware of the woman's abusive behaviour. She was a drug addict and an alcoholic. She always had a full house of children of all ages. I believed she was trying to encourage my children to drink and smoke. Concerned, I notified the police and alerted Social Services. This was after Caitlin stole my family allowance book and cashed it. I reported it to the police to teach Caitlin an invaluable lesson, hoping that it would put the fear of God into her.

But Caitlin rebelled even more and carried on visiting this woman's house, trying her best to conceal it, but we always found out eventually! We kept trying to keep her away, taking away privileges, imposing sanctions, yet nothing deterred her. She turned into the teenager from hell. We moved away 2 years later and things improved for a little while, but this experience had set her on the road to self-destruction.

Eventually though, she started work at the hospital as a ward clerk. She met Lucas's father, Joel, while going on nights out with work colleagues. I was so proud of her when she reached this milestone. I thought this was going to be a turning point in her life. But the relationship with Joel was over before it had even begun. Caitlin was 6 weeks pregnant and she was devastated, as she was completely enamoured by Joel. I wasn't aware at that time but Joel was cheating. He already had a girlfriend who was pregnant. She is now his wife, and one of their three children is the same age as Lucas.

Caitlin took the break-up badly. Thankfully, she was living at home with us and I was there to support her through the separation. But then there was bad news. At the hospital they said her baby would be born with a cleft lip and palate. We had never heard of this birth defect, so we looked it up on the internet to get a better understanding. We had no idea what lay ahead.

I was concerned about Caitlin's continued drinking. I'd had my suspicions from very early on, but when I asked her friends, they would tell me she was just an occasional binge drinker. But it got worse. She would arrive for work after really late boozy nights out. She drank throughout her pregnancy. To be perfectly honest, I never knew the extent of danger that drinking during pregnancy posed to the unborn child, although I knew instinctively it wasn't the best thing to do. I don't think she was ever officially advised against the dangers of drinking or how it can affect the unborn foetus.

Birth of Lucas

Caitlin was 19 years old when Lucas was born. It was not easy. Having a firstborn with complex needs was all too much for her to bear. She didn't bond well with him. It was an emotional rollercoaster – she had an overwhelming feeling of guilt due to his cleft palate and she experienced feelings of inadequacy as a mother. The deficiency was more apparent since cleft babies cannot suckle like normal babies. The method she had to master was using a plastic scoop to feed him as opposed to the traditional bottle with a soft teat. Feeding times were a nightmare for Caitlin. She was terrified he may choke! The milk must constantly flow and you had to be very careful not to lose the momentum. It took me some time to master this technique myself.

She was fearful of Lucas waking through the night with reflux choking. This was a regular event. Her worst fear was that he would stop breathing. I moved Lucas into our room to give Caitlin peace of mind. I can understand why she was scared at times – I was terrified, but someone had to stay calm and deal with the harrowing situation. The ambulance was called a few times as the reflux caused him to stop breathing and he became very rigid. This was frightening for all of us, but Caitlin did improve over time.

While on maternity leave from her job Caitlin was itching to spread her wings. She was making excuses to see friends, asking us to babysit on a regular basis just to get out of the house. But then she would disappear and turn up a few days later after a bender. Occasionally I had to take time off work due to Caitlin disappearing. Things got really difficult. She was drinking until she was unconscious at times, causing many heated arguments. We tried our hardest to make her face up to her responsibilities but bickering got us nowhere. She would push the boundaries and test us greatly.

Caitlin had a [specialised] cleft palate social worker for Lucas to give her support and to work through the techniques to handle different situations. I confided my worst fears to the worker but she just said, 'It's going to take time for her to adapt. It's a distressing time for a young mum of a cleft baby to deal with. Just keep supporting her the best you can and try to step back and let her do more with Lucas.' Eventually she pulled away and left me to do everything, and obviously I couldn't do it all. Lucas had his first cleft repair operation at 10 months old, and she realised that he would have to face more repair operations in the future. She was terrified all the time that something could happen to Lucas, and I think these feelings contributed to making her drinking spiral out of control.

Living with us afforded Caitlin to save up a substantial amount of money, and she decided she wanted to get a place of her own. I was reluctant for her to go, but Lucas was over 2 years by this time, and he was a happy, thriving little boy. I thought to myself maybe it could be a good thing for Caitlin to face her responsibilities head on and bond closer with Lucas without having me and Grandad around.

When she got her own place to live I must admit I did have reservations. I worried how she was coping. I called to her house almost every day. I would use any excuse to see Lucas. I collected him after work from the day nursery and brought him to ours for tea to share a couple of hours with Nana and Grandad. Lucas was used to seeing us last thing at night and first thing in the morning. I tried to withdraw slowly, knowing he would be missing us as much as we were missing him. But Lucas would scream when we dropped him back home and this really used to distress me. Much later, at CAMHS [Child and Adolescent Mental Health Services] they said that due to me taking care of him in his early life, Lucas would have took me for his mum not his nana, and my daughter more like a sister. That's why he got so upset when I dropped him home to Mum's each night. They called it 'attachment disorder'. This really shocked and upset me: when I realised that Lucas would have felt so abandoned and unhappy with this huge change.

Six weeks after moving into her new home, Caitlin met this new man, Kenny, and he moved in with her without us knowing. I met him briefly and wasn't impressed. I felt it was too soon for her to get involved with anyone. Lucas was the most important person in her life and I pleaded with her to get him out. They had just moved into a new house and Lucas needed to be settled. I said, 'Concentrate on cementing the bond with Lucas and building a life together. Lucas needs to get to know you, without strangers coming and going. Please get that sorted before starting a relationship with Kenny.' She didn't listen. A few months later we got the news Caitlin was expecting a second baby. Lee was born in 2008.

The honeymoon period didn't last long. It was soon evident Kenny was beating her – she had black eyes and bruises all over her body during and after her pregnancy. He wrecked her house on many occasions. I found he was a drug addict and so too was his family. I'm not sure how much violence Lucas witnessed but it must have been a terrifying time for the little fella. Caitlin was putting up with serious domestic violence. Kenny controlled her – his violent outbursts included threatening her with knives, humiliating her and making her believe he would come after her family. He would wreck and throw her belongings, smash crockery and make holes in doors. Then he threw her down the stairs and broke her leg. It was a very serious break, meaning she had a full cast from the top of her leg to her foot. Next time she had a hospital appointment she took a friend to help her with the children. On their way home they took a short cut through the park, her on crutches. Kenny appeared, like a bad penny. She told him to leave her alone but then he kicked the crutches from under her and started booting her repeatedly while she was lying on the ground. Luckily for her some Asian guys were passing and pulled him off.

Kenny never left her alone. He would turn up causing trouble at her place of work, so eventually she lost her job. He was not fit to be around children as he did not care who was in the firing line. Caitlin was once cradling Lee in her arms when he knocked both of them to the floor. It took her all her time to stop Lee from falling – this is how crazy this guy was. No one could be sure whether or not the baby hit his head. She made a statement as usual but retracted it soon after. This is how he got away with it. The police were at her door often due to their constant fall-outs, and they notified Social Services and then contacted me. I voiced my own concerns and they advised that Caitlin would have to keep the violent partner away, and asked that I keep constantly checking out the situation. Kenny left, but shortly after, like on previous occasions, Caitlin allowed him back.

And then, before I knew it, the Social Services arrived at my door with Lucas and Lee. I went into panic mode, not to mention shock. I was working full-time; how could I possibly manage this without notice and planning? I was also so ashamed, angry and upset that Caitlin had let it get this far. I found it very difficult to separate the two needs – my grandchildren's and my daughter's. Who was going to support my daughter to unravel her messed-up life?! I was told it would be short term until they got something sorted. Don't get me wrong – I understand why the children were taken, but initially I thought they reacted too quickly. I asked, 'Can't you make it one night?' Give her the chance to sober up and reflect on the seriousness of the consequences she was now facing. Is there no such place as a safe house for her and the boys, so that they wouldn't be separated, until workers decide the best course of action? Somewhere she could be supported and kept a watchful eye over and be taught some valuable parental skills? Sadly, such a place didn't exist, and from that moment my life changed forever. The boys came with just the clothes they were wearing. However, the Social Services did provide a cot for Lee. Every time I asked about what the plans were, they were very evasive. They knew what they wanted – they wanted to leave the children with me. Looking back it was apparent they had a hidden agenda. They wanted free child care, not caring we could be left financially disadvantaged.

I carried on working, but ended up having to get a childminder for the boys. My eldest daughter helped, but she had three boys, her youngest more or less the same age as Lee. As the days went into weeks my daughter asked, 'Mum, how long is this going to go on?' She just couldn't manage. Social Services then stepped up to pay for a registered childminder. I was reluctant to leave them with strangers after all they'd been through. But I had no choice and found a minder close to where I lived. Still it was a very desperate situation. I found my working hours hard to juggle with caring for two very demanding and needy boys. I would get home, sort their tea out, shovel food down, bathe, then bed, only to face the same situation day after day. This went on for months. Luckily my employer was very sympathetic and was flexible enough to work round my situation, due to the length of service I had with them.

Lee didn't really know me as well as Lucas, and of course Caitlin reacted badly to losing the boys. She would drop in when she felt like it, having difficult outbursts. The situation would get very heated and we would fight. Caitlin was emotionally, verbally and physically abusive towards me. When she was fuelled with alcohol she would try to take the boys and threaten to kill herself. It got so serious I had to call the police. They placed handcuffs on her, arrested and removed her. Sadly Lucas witnessed this, which was so distressing, it tore me apart. I got bombarded with nasty, threatening phone calls both at work and at home at all times of the day and night. She'd be screaming and ranting in drink down the phone. Constant threats – if she wasn't going to get her children then she would make sure I wasn't. I wasn't eating or sleeping properly and I lost a lot of weight constantly worrying, walking around in a daze.

In the end I was made redundant when the firm outsourced to China, after working 25 years. It was a great company. I'd been a specification administrator earning £18,500 per annum. I loved my job and was very career-minded so I was shocked. I managed to find another position as a receptionist working for a media group, but then I had to give it up. Who was I kidding? Caring for the boys and working full-time for 8 months until I left almost killed me. I made the decision to put the boys first and stop working. This meant a loss of income for us. I wasn't getting any allowance for the boys – only the monthly child benefit of £82 each.

After doing research on the web I came across the Family Rights Group and started reading the stories of other grandparents in the same situation as us. I came across the term 'kinship carer'. This came with a foster allowance. I questioned the boys' social worker, who told me I could not apply for kinship carer as we had undertaken a private agreement to care for the boys. I couldn't believe what I was hearing! No such conversation ever took place – we were told at the time of placement it would be short term! How dare they twist the truth! No one was looking after our interest, only the interests of the children. Surely they should look after both parties? And there is all the personal interference you have to endure – my life was an open book when caring for the boys. A heated argument followed and the social worker left. With no one to turn to, having no one to offer sound good advice, I got on the phone to Family Rights. They were so helpful. They told me to act quickly, explaining that the authorities were breaking the law. They advised that I needed to request in writing to be assessed as the boys' kinship carer. They provided a pre-written letter with a few blanks that I had to fill in and post out to the manager who worked for the Local Authority.

It took a year of many disagreements before the decision was made to start the process. We had to attend a foster panel where, fortunately for us, we were recognised and accepted as the boys' foster carers. We were assigned our very own social worker and began to be paid an allowance. Thankfully this made up a bit for my loss of income, but the experience of having my own social worker was short lived. The worker only lasted three visits and over time I did without one, even though that worker is supposed to be looking out solely for us.

Living with the Grandchildren

It's really hard and tiring at our age to be taking on the responsibility of three children. The boys' social workers only see a snapshot of your life, and most social workers leave you feeling that they think it's the grandparents' fault and we should just deal with it. Lucas's always been a challenge – he was never tired! He'd never sleep unless he slept in my bed. I had to sleep with the light on and he constantly wet the bed. He'd be really vague sometimes, as if he wasn't there. He couldn't follow instructions very well. Social Services arranged for him to go to CAMHS. Lee had night terrors – he still has them now. Initially I didn't realise what was going on. I thought they were just really naughty children. But I knew something was not right.

Forced to give up work to care for the children, I had to grieve the loss of my social life. Friends became very thin on the ground. You stop getting invited out. People stop visiting you. We're the same age but their children have all grown up and they don't really want to be around younger screaming children. I felt isolated and lonely and I pushed everyone away. I was jealous, seeing and hearing about friends and family having wonderful holidays or evenings out! The life I once knew had come to an abrupt end! My relationship with my husband suffered. We had limited time together anyway, due to him working away from home (he was a long-distance lorry driver). When he was home the time was consumed by caring for the boys and when the days were over we just wanted to collapse in bed. There was no time for us to be alone or even leave the house on our own to have time together. There were times when I felt like walking out and not coming back. I was also concerned that time was running out for my daughter. Her lifestyle not changing, not showing enough improvement, never moving forward, just backwards – ruining any chance of getting her children back. I love my grandsons so much but my stress level sometimes got the better of me. I found myself thinking of all the things that I could do if they did not live here. Then I just sat and cried for having those thoughts.

Meanwhile my daughter missed many reviews. Her needs seemed more important than the boys and her life appeared like one big party. She never sought help to address her mental health or emotional problems. Things went downhill. For a time, she lost contact with the whole family and lived rough in desperate conditions. She was still on and off with her abusive boyfriend, but now evicted from her home and flitting from house to house of so-called friends. She would sleep anywhere. One day she came home drunk and so difficult that me and the boys' social worker tried to get her sectioned under the Mental Health Act. I was hoping they would help her to address her issues and get rid of her monsters and demons once and for all. But they said she was 'quite normal, just an alcoholic'. Meanwhile I realised that she had become used to her freedom without her babies. Occasionally people told me stories that I'd rather not hear – usually another beating suffered at Kenny's hands – that guy that called himself her boyfriend. This guy not only controlled her, he brainwashed her. He was relentless. I was off my head with worry about what might happen to her: would I get that dreaded phone call in the middle of the night that something terrible had happened to my daughter as a result of him?

By 2009 Caitlin was pregnant for the third time with Joshua, but Social Services placed a Child Protection Order on him even before he was born. Out of fear of losing her third child, Caitlin at long last made a conscious decision to cooperate with social workers. They got her a flat not far from my house and Caitlin agreed to take out an injunction and keep well away from her abusive partner. Joshua was born in 2010. The social workers made her have regular blood tests to check on her alcohol intake and they would call without warning to make sure she wasn't drinking. She started to see me and her other two boys on a regular basis, which was good for all the boys and ensured they were around their new baby brother. I thought this was great: a turning point; a chance for her to pick herself up and turn her life around. I tried to distance myself from baby Joshua because I did not want to get too emotionally attached this time. Deep down I knew something could go wrong but I stepped back and hoped Caitlin would step up and be a mother. During their visits I saw that Caitlin was taking good care of Joshua. He was clean and well fed. This was the moment I had always dreamed of. How wonderful to see my daughter bonding for the very first time with one of her children!

Caitlin convinced me that she was doing everything right – that she was cooperating, not drinking and not seeing her abusive partner. But it turned out that the 'fresh start' was far from the truth. When Joshua was 18 month old, Social Services suddenly announced that they were going to court to get him adopted! I'm thinking they can't possibly do this! She's *doing* what she should be doing. Firstly they asked me if *I* could look after Joshua. I thought, 'Oh no, here we go again!' I didn't think it possible to take a third child, and they didn't tell me all they knew. If they had been straight and given me all the facts, I would have taken Joshua in an instant. I didn't realise the enormity of the case file on Caitlin in this new situation.

In Court

I still believed nothing would come of it. Caitlin had been doing so well taking care of Joshua, and I saw her most days. I attended court to support Caitlin. She only came once – she couldn't face it. To my horror the evidence presented on Caitlin was mostly supplied by Kenny, her abusive partner, whom I knew would do anything to destroy her. He produced phone texts to show they were still having a relationship – this was extremely damning for my daughter. It became apparent that Caitlin had still been seeing him after Joshua was born, even though he was under a Restraining Order. He had even been to her flat occasionally. It unfolded that police were called on two occasions after he attacked her! Why was I so blind? I had seen bruises, but when I questioned her she brushed them off by telling me she'd got them moving heavy furniture around in her flat. At that moment I felt sick to my stomach and became very scared for Joshua. This was serious.

The Cafcass [Children and Family Court Advisory and Support Service] court guardian took me to a room and told me Joshua will be going up for adoption. I was so upset and in a state of shock. I said I never expected this. If they'd told me the evidence gathered on Caitlin and been upfront, this nightmare wouldn't be happening. I would have took Joshua without question. The guardian said that the only way to stop Joshua going up for adoption was for us to take him under a Residency Order, which could be agreed today. To my horror she went on to say that the authorities wanted stability for the older siblings too and, therefore, I would have to take either Residence or Special Guardianship Orders [SGOs] on them too, and that I would no longer be their kinship foster carer. I would need a solicitor to act on our behalf. My whole world was falling apart. Not fully understanding what was happening, terrified what this meant for us, I wanted to scream. I felt betrayed and pushed towards what the establishment so hypocritically suggest is in the 'best interests of the children'. It was not just about Joshua. There was no concern for what this would mean for all our needs.

I was forced to agree to the Residence Order on Joshua, and the judge then adjourned the case. I was falling apart and meanwhile Joshua was placed to stay with us later that day! There were only a few days before the next hearing, though the authorities did agree to pay the solicitors' fees for us to go to court. With my husband away so much at work, I was on my own with the overwhelming pressure, the enormity, panic and worry of having to arrange for a solicitor – how was I going to manage this? I arrived home with Joshua and broke down in floods of tears. Where do

I start? Which solicitor do I call? I went online and blindly took the first one I came across. No time to seek some good advice or check reviews. I didn't even have enough time to give them a proper history of the case or explain why I wanted to stop Joshua going up for adoption, and that at the hearing I'd agreed to accept a Residency Order. Two days flew by. I hardly slept, didn't eat and was off my head with worry. Things were out of control.

Meanwhile I'm also trying to cope with Joshua – it was a nightmare situation. He'd really bonded with his mummy, so it was extremely hard and upsetting for him as an 18-month-old child. I was under immense stress.

Then [because Joshua was being considered for adoption] the social worker made arrangements for him to be checked out by a specialist on foetal alcohol spectrum disorder (FASD) – a consultant paediatrician. I didn't have a clue as to what FASD meant, until after I had a consultation with the specialist. The social worker was late and we started without her. On first glance at Joshua she said it looked to her that he had the facial characteristics of this disorder. After some history and further checks, she diagnosed him as having FASD. She gave me leaflets and suggested I read up on it. When I was told it was alcohol-related, I said, 'Well, Caitlin drank with all three boys.' I gave the paediatrician a brief history regarding the other two siblings, and of course she asked why they had not been referred as well. When the social worker arrived, I was straight to the point asking that very question. 'Why have you arranged for only Joshua to be checked out by the specialist? Why not his other two siblings?' They knew the mother drank alcohol with all three boys. The social worker was reluctant to respond and I said 'I want you to arrange an appointment for all three boys to be checked.'

After doing my own investigations I figured social workers must have had suspicions about the harmful effect Caitlin's alcohol abuse could have inflicted on her three children, but they never mentioned or discussed it with me. The only reason they were acting now and required a health screen on Joshua was because they wanted to put him up for adoption. I repeatedly asked the social worker, 'When will my two other grandchildren be tested?' But before I knew it, we were at court.

On the day of the hearing, my barrister took me into a room and advised that, despite my pleas, the authority's care plans for Lucas and Lee were to move them to Special Guardianship Orders. They were looking for 'permanency' for all three boys. In the family court the Residency Order (without payment) was confirmed for Joshua, and a hearing date set for applications to the court for SGOs for Lucas and Lee. Of course I was relieved that Joshua was no longer up for adoption, to be raised by strangers. But now we had to go back to court and fight again for Lucas and Lee. Now the authorities sang our praises, saying that I and my husband had done a wonderful job bringing up the older siblings for the last 4 years but that the children needed stability and that we should become Special Guardians. They expected to just walk away and leave us to it when we needed the financial and other support which we would lose if they were on SGOs. We wanted to continue as kinship carers. They never took into consideration the challenges that faced us every day in view of Joshua's latest diagnosis of FASD, and pending a follow-up appointment for his older two siblings, who might have the same diagnosis! The barrister I had acting on my behalf wasn't very good. I would have done better acting on behalf of myself, but to be fair, he didn't know enough about our case history and had only a very short time to prepare and plan.

Although we never sought Special Guardianship Orders it was the authority's intention to thrust them upon us! I made the decision to seek better legal representation. The court guardian name-dropped a good family lawyer that would be paid for by the authorities. Before the next court appearance the authorities had to start building their case regarding Lucas and Lee. I wasn't on good terms with the boy's social worker as this was the fourth worker we had the pleasure to get involved with. We never had a permanent worker during the whole time caring for the boys so never had the opportunity to build a rapport with one. Knowing court was imminent, Social Services arranged for a new social worker to push and prepare us to accept Special Guardianship Orders.

A Family Group Conference was arranged to discuss what support my own wider family could provide while we continued to care for the boys. While agreeing to this meeting, I knew already what support my family could offer me was limited – they had their own family commitments, coupled with work. I didn't want to burden them, making them feel obliged and increasing the pressures in their lives. I said that what I need is to have transparency and to speak to other grandparents in the same situation as us! It was then the Family Group Conference worker told me about the Bridge Project and support group involving other grandparents. It took 5 years for me to get this information, as I had repeatedly asked about organisations like this and was told that no such group existed nearby. Some time later I got a letter from the Family Group Conference thanking us for our cooperation, and agreeing they could perhaps have put some help in place had they been involved at the very beginning when we first started caring for the boys.

Meanwhile my solicitor's junior was preparing our case ready for court while the authorities prepared their case. A few months later the solicitor forwarded us a copy of the authority's ready-prepared statement for the court hearing. I could not believe some of what I was reading. They claimed we were not fully cooperating. And then there is our whole life history exposed, but with so many facts missing, or wrong. What was hard to accept was that the court guardian had taken the side of the authorities. This news was soul-destroying and would not stand us in good stead! Our solicitor asked me to prepare my statement for court and return it for them to grammatically correct and improve it in lawyers' terms. My statement went back and forth for amendments as I kept banging on about things that they thought were trivial but to me were important details. I was insistent regarding the pending appointment for the older children. Months had passed and still no paediatrician appointment. But the court hearing only lasted three-quarters of an hour and it was adjourned as the judge wanted the SGO care plans in place before judgement.

Six weeks later we were back in court, but at least this time we had a more senior barrister to speak for us. We had a little talk from him explaining that this case could be a precedent in law regarding issuing SGOs to grandparents who did not seek one, as in our case. This made me more nervous as I saw it carried more weight than before. The authority's barrister had got the SGO plans prepared for our case. They put their case forward; so too did our barrister. Our barrister stressed it was vital we received an appointment for Lucas and Lee to find out whether or not they had the same condition as Joshua. Our barrister described the challenges we would be facing if all three boys were to have the same condition and how the care plans did not reflect this possible situation. It's the most horrible experience to be present and hear everyone is talking about you as if you were invisible, and not be able to argue back! Devastatingly for us, the judge's decision was to award Special Guardianship Orders for Lucas and Lee as well as Joshua. The judge's summing-up emphasised that if Lucas and Lee continued under [Kinship] Care Orders they would feel disparities with Joshua, who was under a Special Guardianship Order. I thought, 'That's rubbish. That's not going to change anything. Why would they feel different – it's just a piece of paper!' The same love, energy and compassion would be bestowed on all, and they wouldn't understand until they're a little older. I felt so let down by the system. So alone, no one on our side. I couldn't take anything in, everything was a blur. Our barrister was as disappointed and shocked as us. He advised us to appeal this decision, but it would be at cost to us – around £5000!

After leaving court I felt numb. I think they'd just looked at the fact that we are caring people and that we'd be able to manage. But it's essential you can keep and support the children. We would be losing the Family and Friends foster care allowances as well as the built-in support from professionals who are present during reviews. They are there to ensure the best action when needed for health, education and well-being for your children. And my children had so many needs!

I just survived after that. Some days I just wanted to cry all day. I didn't want to go anywhere because I couldn't take any more happy families. I tried to keep my emotions in check around the boys, but it was really difficult. I was seething with anger at what had happened. I felt this was wrong. I felt I was being punished. But slowly I got my fighting spirit back and phoned the solicitor. I couldn't accept what I felt to be an injustice or allow the court to decide what's best for my grandchildren. I said we would appeal, though it was an awful amount of money to contemplate losing. Then, about 8 weeks later, a surprise! I was informed by our solicitor that the appeal costs would be taken care of by legal aid. Perhaps my luck was changing. Again we had to prepare from scratch.

New statements had to be prepared and I insisted on more control this time. I channelled all my energy into reading all the revised Special Guardianship, support and final care plans in respect of Lee and Lucas so I could respond. I highlighted all the incorrect details in the authority's reports regarding our life history, just to emphasise how little notice they had taken of what we had said during our interviews. The solicitor now included every addition I insisted on.

Then another twist of fate occurred. The long-awaited consultation with the paediatrician took place. Sadly, all three boys were diagnosed with the same condition, FASD, and the problems they would have were spelt out. Because of the 'prenatal alcohol exposure', our grandchildren would have 'cognitive and behavioural problems'. The brains of children with FASD are wired differently, so they are impulsive, hyperactive and easily distractable. They have poor social skills, difficulty understanding cause and effect, lack of conscience, and learning difficulties. It was devastating news.

Part of the court process is that the Cafcass guardian had to visit us for a statement. She asked many questions regarding the boys, including this new information about FASD. A week before we went to court the guardian came over to our side. This was great news for us though we could not understand why she hadn't stood by us the whole time! Anyway we went to appeal and were distressed when in court the authority's barrister said that we were not at all cooperative in accepting the Family Group Conference proposals. Fortunately I was more prepared this time and had the letter from the Family Group Conference organisers with me. I nudged my barrister and passed the letter to him. He interrupted the proceedings to disagree with the statement of the Local Authority's barrister. The letter was copied and passed to the judge. That felt so good and gave credence to how many more untruths were reported. I also played an instrumental part with regards to my statement and my persistence and determination to have my say. I was so relieved and happy when the SGOs were changed.

Lucas and Lee were transferred back to Foster Care Orders, though we had to return to panel to be approved again as Family and Friends carers. We didn't understand why, but Joshua was transferred from a Residency Order to an SGO but still without any financial award at first. The authorities were advised by the judge to arrange long-awaited respite for myself and my husband. After almost 5 years of caring we might at last get some time alone to recharge.

I was on top of the world after the verdict. The immense pressure I was under released like a pressure cooker. This great joy happened in time for us to really celebrate Christmas. The previous Christmas had been ruined as I was emotionally and physically drained after losing the case when the SGOs were imposed on us.

At last I was offered 8 months of limited respite using a charitable organisation. However, they tried to exclude Joshua because he was under a Special Guardianship Order. I stood my ground, saying the boys come as a package and how upset and different Joshua would feel having to stay at home while his brothers went off for a sleepover. Eventually they agreed to include him. They come Friday evening and take two of the three boys until the following day, when they collect the third for a day-out altogether. Each week they took different boys for the sleepover. This works, but getting them ready is a lot of added stress and I still don't get time to myself.

Caitlin's Death and the Aftermath

Meanwhile, Caitlin got worse. She got a lot worse, after losing Joshua. She just went right down. The boys would be lucky if they saw her every 4 weeks, and they would feel let down and upset when she failed to turn up. But then I noticed she was poorly a lot. And she wasn't eating. And what happened, she collapsed, she went to hospital and they told her that her liver was failing and if she didn't stop drinking it would kill her. She ran off without treatment – she couldn't face the enormity of what was said to her. Unknown to us, in 2010 after Joshua was born Caitlin was warned to take better care and cut down her alcohol intake, but like lots of young people, she never thought it would happen to her. Well, Caitlin's death shows it can happen.

One day in November 2014 the weather was bitter, teeming down with rain. Caitlin came knocking on the door. She was sobbing and looked so gaunt and afraid. She asked to come in to bathe and apply medicines prescribed by her doctor. I was taken aback and shocked when I saw the state of her body. She was covered in this horrific angry rash which looked like she had been burnt in a fire. I ran a nice hot bath for her and asked her to give me a shout when she needed me to apply the cream. It took me all my strength to fight back the tears so as not to alarm her further. I insisted on going to the doctors that evening with her. I needed to find out what was wrong with her. I was mortified to hear that Caitlin had been dealing with this rash for a few weeks, causing her to miss a very important appointment with the liver specialist. I was expecting the doctor to send her straight to hospital. He tried contacting the liver specialist while we were both present but unsuccessfully. He said he will continue to try to contact him for an emergency appointment – in the meantime just go home and continue with the medicine. I got angry with the doctor and said, 'That's not good enough', but in the end I had no option but to bring her home as she needed someone to look after her. Her flat was not fit for purpose, not for a person presenting with such horrific symptoms and not having the means to pay for lighting or heating. When we got home she said, 'I feel like I'm dying.' By the next day she was worse, and I called an ambulance and she was admitted into hospital.

Each day that passed caused me further distress, anxiety and concern. I could see my daughter wasting away at death's door. Three consultants seemed unable to help her, and 15 days passed without her eating. She was in immense pain and couldn't tolerate anyone touching her. One consultant seemed to have no empathy or compassion, blaming her for not cooperating. To us she was precious, not just another patient on the conveyor belt. It wasn't right she should have to suffer in this way. I wish I had stood up to them sooner, but they make you feel ashamed – them knowing she was alcoholic – as if she got what she deserved. But alcohol dependency is a devastating disease. During and after visits I was left inconsolably upset and distressed. I could not sleep.

Her other organs began to fail and we were more or less told that she was dying. She was moved to the High Dependency Unit. It was the day before Christmas Eve and she was sedated. For the first time in hospital I felt relieved. Caitlin looked comfortable and at peace and I felt she was in the arms of angels. I believe she should have been sent to intensive care long before they eventually did. Next day a feeding drip was at last administered, coupled with an intravenous drip to administer antibiotics for sepsis and much-needed morphine for the pain. I was happy that my daughter was finally getting the care she so deserved.

By Christmas Day a crucial 48 hours had passed and we were still left with some hope. We went to visit Caitlin. She seemed more alert but was confused and a little aggressive, trying all the time to remove her oxygen mask, constantly trying to talk through the mask, telling us that she loved us, reaching her arms out. I tried to calm her by explaining that she was in special care, and, 'Now we need you to concentrate on getting better.' Telling her that the boys missed her and sent their love! Telling her the boys enjoyed opening their presents. I don't think she had any idea that it was Christmas. I didn't want to leave, but we had three excited little boys that were unaware of what was happening with their mummy. They just wanted to celebrate Christmas. Then at 4am we received that dreaded call. I knew instantly when that phone rang what I was about to be told. The nurse told us we should come in as soon as possible but Caitlin sadly passed away within 10 minutes. It was so sudden and we never got chance to say goodbye.

When she passed away a piece of us went missing. My one and only wish had been that one day the boys would be reunited with their mum and now that dream was shattered. With a heavy heart I decided not to let the boys attend the funeral. I wanted to shield them from all that sadness and allow them to remember happy times spent here with Mum. We sent balloons off with attached messages to heaven for Mummy. Our intention is to continue and mark her yearly anniversary in this way.

Looking Forward

I was surprised to see Lucas's father at the funeral. I was even more surprised when he offered his hand in support and requested to play a part in Lucas's life! Initially I was suspicious of what his intentions might be and certainly would not agree to him taking Lucas away – our family is the only family they've ever known and can depend on. Gladly he was not suggesting this, but Lucas's father had never been involved, and Lucas had missed out on having relatives on that side. For that reason I agreed to allow him to get to know his father. Unfortunately, contact between Lucas and his father upset his other two siblings. They are jealous – they want to see *their* daddy! But their father is in prison for manslaughter, after nearly killing someone. I've tried to be as honest as possible with the children, explaining that Daddy is in prison for doing a really bad thing and it will be a very long time before they see him again. Then they wanted to see *Lucas's* daddy – 'Why can't we go?' They hate the fact of one having something and not the other. I am trying to find a way. They will get curious as they get older, seeking answers to so many questions.

I feel more protective towards the boys since they lost their mummy. I feel I've turned into a constant nagging parent, and nobody wants their grandchildren to remember them in that way. And the older the boys get, the harder life becomes. They're always wanting this and that, not to mention having to join every activity going, like the football – I mean when you have to stand out in the freezing cold while they practise or play, it's horrible!

The boy's behaviour can change on a day-to-day basis with their condition. They really test you. In and out of bed, not sleeping, running round like cowboys and Indians, bickering and fighting. However, after they were diagnosed I was so relieved and thankful that it was not just down to naughty behaviour. They were prescribed melatonin for sleep and it has made such a difference to us after suffering so many sleepless nights over a long period of time. My quality of life – and the boys' – has improved as a result.

Routines for the boys are a must. If you relax them slightly you're in trouble. They're all very demanding, very impulsive. They can get so hyperactive when people visit, or anything outside of the normal routine is happening. You can never relax. They can be very moody. One minute they're happy, silly, helpful and loving everybody and everything. In another mood they can get very angry, stomp feet, hit siblings and so on. These moods can shift many times in the day. Lee especially has a very short fuse. While bickering with his brothers he will pick things up and throw them without thinking. It's so scary. A little frustration about something sets him off into the yelling, angry, door-slamming mood. We make him take time out while he calms down. If he yells at us, or hits, kicks or throws and breaks things, this is unacceptable and we will sanction him by cutting his allowance.

You can give only one instruction at a time. If I say, 'Finish that biscuit, then go brush your teeth', Lucas will confuse the two things and brush his teeth first then finish the biscuit! They constantly lose things like coats, hats, gloves and their toys around the house. They forget things so easily. We use visual timetables to remind them and aid them to cope with everyday life. Consistency is key as they make the same mistakes over and over again. But at times it is really exhausting, so repetitive hearing the tiresome echo of your own voice. Lucas can be orally fixated, putting anything and everything into his mouth! They all have problems with dressing, often putting clothing on inside out or backwards way round, although they are getting better with age. Lee is doing well in school, though – better than his brothers, who have some learning difficulties. They do get on, but the older they get, the more sibling rivalry there is. There's a lot of jealousy between them.

Thinking about the future can be frightening. If something serious happened to us our wish is that the boys would be kept together and not separated. I'm 59 years old now. Apart from stress, thankfully I'm not in bad health yet, but I worry. I'd like to think that my son or daughter will step up and take them on. I truly believe they would, but you can't be too sure. I do occasionally broach the subject because I'd feel much happier, knowing the boys will always be kept together with their extended family.

The best advice I can give to others in this position is just survive and get through it. There are no magic formulas. A lot of self-belief and pushing onwards and upwards. You go through so much pain. But just know that you are not alone, but that you can, you will and you must just survive for the children. Our grandchildren have become the most precious thing in our lives. I do not know what I would do without them now. I do think you learn more patience once you've been through all this, though cruelly we lost so much. You've more understanding. And obviously you've changed and you mellow, and get more wisdom. And there are rewards – seeing the children meeting their milestones, their happy smiling faces that melt your heart. Now I feel more secure – it's knowing that we're going to be able to provide for them, whereas before that would have been the biggest worry.

* * *

Editorial Commentary

Grandparents taking on one grandchild in these adverse circumstances can stretch them almost beyond endurance, but to have to take on *three*, all with special needs, is an amazing achievement. Like many of us, Shelly had little knowledge of the impact of substance addiction, but she has fought to learn and to get help against a wall of denial of her and the children's needs.

Self-blame when a child turns to substance abuse in their adolescence is common to most parents, together with the fear that the world will judge them harshly. Frequently parents struggle to prevent a slide into drinking or use of drugs, at the point when young people most resist parental controls and are striving to assert their independence. Pregnancy in these circumstances can be an added blow that neither the young person nor their parents anticipate, and when it is sometimes too late to stop the chemical clock of addiction from ticking to destruction – as happened in this case when drink eventually led to death.

Having the first two children 'dumped' on Shelly and her husband – with a misleading promise that it would be 'short term', and no assessment of how the grandparents were to manage when both of them worked – echoes other stories we have told. This was later presented as 'a private arrangement', enabling the Local Authority to resist Shelly's initial bid to become a kinship carer.

Unlike the other grandparents, who have eventually found a way of legalising their independent control over the future of their troubled grandchildren, Shelly eventually made a sensible calculation that she could not survive without financial and material support if these children were to thrive. Others have taken Residence Orders or Special Guardianships, which do not guarantee funding, whilst of course most grandparents act informally and have no legal status at all.

Becoming a kinship carer (in effect an employee of the local council) should mean that Shelly has access to professional help as well as funding. It is hard to imagine an impartial observer thinking she did not need such support. But instead of it being delivered as a right, she had to fight for it in court, in an adversarial setting, up against the Local Authority. She even had to pay part of the legal costs herself, despite her limited circumstances. That it came 'right' in the end is no tribute to this system.

It is evident from this case that Social Services have little understanding of the impact of substance abuse on physical and intellectual development. It is only when they acted to have one of her grandchildren adopted that a statutory medical intervention disclosed his FASD condition. Even then, Shelly had to battle to have the other two children assessed.

Like the other grandparents in this book, Shelly has done an incredible job – despite extreme isolation, losing her employment, her marriage being under pressure and an uncertain future ahead. She has learnt to manage the symptoms of children with FASD with consistent routines and reassurance, and, whilst she is sometimes at the end of her tether, she does not give up.

Mary Womersley

'The grandchildren are our future'

Mary was the convenor of The Grandparents Group, which she set up more than 10 years ago as part of her job as carer support worker at the Bridge Drug Centre. Bitter personal experience led her to understand the need of grandparents with substance-misusing children for a space where they could support each other and find solace and understanding. Despite her inspired service, she recently had to take redundancy when public funding was cut. This account was written just before she left in mid-2015.

* * *

I'd had some upsetting experiences with my own family around substance misuse and I went to Bridge for some help. And then in 1997 I helped, as a volunteer, to set up the carers' service. I was trained in-house at counselling skills, trained fully about substance abuse, then, as I spoke to clients as a volunteer, I started to hear about the impact on their lives.

Then I decided on my own to go to night school. I went for a year to Bradford College, and I got my counselling diploma. I loved it, and I wanted to go for the degree. I'd always wanted to be a social worker. But it would have cost me £8000 and I couldn't afford it.

You don't stay for ever as a volunteer, so I'd left Bridge, and then in 2004 I saw this job advertised – carers' support worker at the Bridge Project, supporting families. I decided to go for it. I had the training and because I've experienced it myself, the empathy was obviously there too. When I got it, I was delighted. For 6 months there had been nobody working in the carers' service – it was neglected completely. So I had to literally go in and start that service again myself. The director and the manager suggested I did some group training. So I went to Brighton for 4 days. And later on I did a nurturing course run by Barnardo's to help people to parent, and I gained more skills and absolutely loved it.

First I had to find ways of letting people know about the carers' service. I started off with GPs, because I was thinking about where families would go for help. I contacted GPs, probation officers, other professionals in the housing services. I went to chemists because mothers pick up prescriptions for users sometimes. I did a presentation to the health visitors and school nurses. In between that, I'd get an odd mother that'd ring up, and then once the workers in Bridge knew I was in place, they started to say, 'We've got somebody that might be able to support *you*.' So people started trickling in. I started to see different types of families – mothers, brothers, aunties, grandparents. I see relatives on a one-to-one basis. Probably about 50 of them by now. I don't see substance misusers. I support anybody who's worried about somebody else's drug use, but they don't use themselves. If they use themselves, they're referred to the main service and are not for me. If a mother comes down to see me, and she brings along the substance misuser, I can't see him at all. The boundaries have got to be extremely clear. But if I see Mum, and the drug worker is seeing her son, we can have a four-way meeting, which I do regular.

Now the staff in Bridge refer clients to me, but some are self-referrals, or a GP could refer someone, or someone from the criminal justice system could refer someone. I get lots of different referrals. You've got parents whose sons or daughters have been using substances for years – hard drugs, cannabis, alcohol and legal highs – mostly young males, but females as well. And they've only just heard about the service. So they've come to see me when they are physically, financially and mentally drained, because no one's told them about the service before that and they're still struggling. I see partners of drug users where there is cocaine use – in particular just recently, people running their own businesses – computers, plumbing, builders. It's usually males, using cocaine to stay awake to keep their business running. Yeah, I've seen that a lot recently.

Numbers are increasing because the carers' service is now well established. A mother will ring up in distress, and say, 'Has my son been in to Bridge, or my daughter?' The staff say, 'We can't give that out.' 'What d'ya mean, you can't give that out? I'm really upset – she's missing and I don't know where she is.' (If the drug user signs a waiver, we can then tell Mum that yes, he has been into Bridge, and the tests are like this.) Eventually the staff say, 'Well, I've got somebody that you can speak to.' 'What do you mean, "speak to"?' Some people – a lot of people – at first say, 'No I don't need it. *I'm* all right: it's *her* (or *him*) that needs help.' I think it's us women are worse. Because we think we're superhuman – and we're not. So the staff say, 'Do *you* need support? Who's looking after *you*?'

I offer initial support sessions to everyone, and every time I see somebody, whoever they are, on the first session there is a box of tissues, lots of tears and disclosure. Some feel guilty, as if they've betrayed the person who's using – 'I'm saying awful things about my son and he can be really nice as well.' But it is a relief to tell someone. If somebody rings up and they're in floods of tears, I try to get them in as soon as possible. After that initial meeting, they know what they're coming into the week after. They're not as tearful – tears are there, but they're not so distressed because I know the story now. In the end, when I've given them some sort of advice and explained what I'm going to do, then at the end I say, 'Have you found this helpful?' And every time they say, 'Yes'. They feel safe and they feel this big weight is lifted. Being listened to without judgement is crucial.

They're coming to see me about their daughter's or son's drug use; however, the issue right now might actually be that the daughter and her children are going to be evicted. So I may have to advocate for them and ring up the housing. I work with other services. I went to see a lady whose son was using drugs. She had just lost her husband, who did everything. Her benefits were in a state, the son was going to get her evicted because of his criminal behaviour and disruption on the street – there were several issues going on. So I had to prioritise – first one was the eviction. I contacted the council who were ordering the eviction. Then I got the benefits on board. And then one of her daughters was pregnant and clearly struggling, so I got a health visitor in. Then with the drug user it was the criminal justice system, so we got *them* on board. Then we had this big multi-agency meeting, to sort all this out. For the mother, who had lost her husband – I rang Bradford Bereavement Support and they got her in for some bereavement counselling.

Or maybe a mother says, 'I give him [drug user] £50 a day.' Okay, then, so let's look at reducing that. But whatever we look at, it's got to be workable for *her* – *I* don't live in that house. It's got to be manageable, it's got to be safe, she's got to be safe, other family members have got to be involved. Sometimes I've seen whole families in the house. I've gone out to see them. Because they've all got to be singing from the same hymn sheet.

I was building this service up for about a year but as we got into 2005, I started to notice something. Clients coming in and saying, 'I'm worried about my daughter's drug use, and I've got my grandchildren.' So I thought, 'This is really hidden!' I'd never given it a thought that this could be happening out there. I just thought these grandparents need to be getting support. So I went to my manager and said, 'Could I run a support group for people who are caring for or have cared for their grandchildren due to substance abuse?' And he said, 'Well, yes, you could.' Later I started other carer groups – one for Asian women only, another for carers struggling with the death of users – a bereavement group. But let me concentrate here on the grandparents.

Setting Up a Support Group for Grandparents

I contacted each of the grandparents and asked them if they'd like a group. Of course, a group is not everyone's cup of tea, and some people had work commitments and couldn't come, but about eight of them said yes. I knew it would work, because they didn't have anything else. They've no support from Social Services – though some have had too much (unhelpful) involvement! They couldn't talk to families or friends – cos they didn't understand. They felt like they were the only ones, looking after these children. And they felt ashamed: 'Look what my daughter's done, or my son.'

They felt guilty: 'I've done something wrong. I don't tell people because they'll judge my daughter. Even though I don't particularly like her at the moment, I don't want anyone else to dislike her. She's got some good qualities. But other people'll judge her, and then they'll look at me, and judge me, because my daughter did this and maybe it's my fault.' So all this! It was *masses* of emotions. Family squabbles, with the other sons and daughters: 'Well you're looking after *her* children – you only see mine on a Saturday! Why do they get a bigger present and mine don't?' So you get all this! So to go to a group, who *totally* understand, immediately, was amazing. Do you know what I loved about it? There was that bond. It's immeasurable really.

We had the first meeting in December 2005. I'll never forget it. I had a flip chart, asking them what they wanted from the group. We had a meeting every month and I minuted every meeting: 'The group felt that they wanted some information about this drug...' and so on. I minuted their needs and that they wanted speakers to come in – from Social Services, a child psychologist, an MP. And I started to learn more about Family Rights Group, the Grandparents' Association – these are groups I never knew existed. I did that for 6 months and then I decided: right, they're established now and it doesn't have to be so formal.

It was so successful that a journalist from the *T&A* [*Telegraph and Argus*] came up and interviewed the group and they published a big piece – no photographs, but they did some case studies. And then the mother of a BBC reporter read the article, told her daughter, they contacted me – from the BBC. Said we want to do a story about the grandparents. I asked the grandparents and they said yes. Only one allowed her full face to be seen, and the rest it was only the lips that they filmed. And then there was a blurred vision of the group behind them. And it actually went on to the *BBC 10 O'Clock News* – it was about 3 minutes.

Going back to the first meeting, though, there were a lot of tears and self-disclosure because of the empathy and that total understanding. There were some stories worse than others and there was a feeling from one or two that 'I thought I had it bad, but…' One of the grandparents who came to the group with his son had *five* of his grandchildren with him! He was in very poor health. His daughter had been living in a flat and she had these five children. When he went to the house with his son, the children were upstairs, no clothes on, people downstairs using drugs; house was all neglected. So they burst into the door, got these children out and took them home to protect them. But Social Services said that because it was a voluntary arrangement, they weren't obliged to help. He lived in a very small house, not equipped for five children, but they wouldn't move him. There was nowhere for the children to put their clothes. Do you know what they gave him? A shed! I was so appalled at a professional level, and a human-being level and a mother and grandmother meself, at how they could have been treated like this! And then he died and the children were spread around the family. It's better than nothing, however – better than being split up. A few of us went to his funeral.

The group did become very close and still are. Several of the members are still coming, after 10 years. One or two have drifted into the group and drifted out again for various reasons. Some people thought, 'It's been brilliant, but I don't need it no more.' At one time it expanded to two groups, but then both groups got a bit smaller and I joined them together again. I think that eight in a group is right – any more and there are certain things that people can't say. Every single meeting of every single group there's never been a minute's silence. So that in itself shows you the need. It was very relaxed – there was none of this, 'Well, your daughter's not using now, go away.' Some people are scared it will happen again – sometimes it does happen.

Facilitating the meeting I always make sure that everybody has spoken and said what they want to say. I don't want anyone going away from the group feeling that they haven't got issues off their chest. Everybody's problem is equally important to be listened and heard, even though some might be less dramatic than others. Sometimes towards the end of a meeting someone has said, 'This or that has happened and we didn't have chance to talk about it', so before they leave I'll say to that person, 'Do you want to give me a call tomorrow and maybe come in and see me?' I don't want them to wait for 4 weeks, for the next meeting.

As a professional I have to keep some distance, which is hard. I've known the group for such a long time – although they are not my friends, I know that much about them. But I always remember that this group is for them, it's not for me. I think that's how I managed to go back to work when my son died. In the group or with clients I just totally focus – what's gone on in my private life is not in my head. Occasionally with clients who've lost somebody I might say, 'I understand, because I have had this experience too.' But it's very rare I do that – obviously you don't want to end up with them counselling you!

In this group I've never seen any arguments, though I saw it once in another carer group when I was a volunteer. It threw me completely. The grandparents are very respectful and caring though, and even in other groups I've never come across that since. The grandparents are often angry, with their children, with the drugs or the dealers, with Social Services. Then I'll use a scenario: for example, hating drug dealers.

I understand what you're saying and I totally understand how you feel, but you know, I've got clients that have actually gone out and said something to a dealer. But that frustration, you know, it's best to let go of that, because firstly it's dangerous – if you are going to do anything, do it anonymously, to the police. It's very dangerous – and if my clients went out and shot 10 dealers, there'd be another 20 round the corner. You know, try to let go of that, it's wasted energy. I know how you feel, but that energy is so wasted. Put that energy back into yourself, you know – let the criminal justice system sort them out – because they *do* sort them out, you see it in the paper every week that they've been caught. So let them get on with that and you concentrate on what you need.

And I do hope that defuses it by giving them an example of other clients. At the same time I think it's healthy and good for them to blurt it out – any emotion – and anger is one we all feel. Get it off your chest in the group, where you're understood. No one's going to say, 'Yeah I know what you mean. Let's go get a gun and kill 'em all.' You know, they're going to understand you. You're going to be allowed to let off that steam, and not be laughed at or judged or anything like that. If the group didn't have that – I kind of think, 'Oh, where would they tek that? And would it get them into any trouble?'

One thing that does bother the group, given their ages, is that death may come too soon. Of course it could be illness – maybe the start of Alzheimer's or rheumatoid arthritis – and you're unable physically to look after the children any more. It's come up so many times in the group. One or two have said they've got a little bit of provision (my daughter, my auntie) but it's not really set in concrete. It bothers me a lot and I have thought of trying to find out who could come in and help us. Maybe a solicitor, or a social worker. What I know is that Social Services are only involved if the child is at risk – and when the parent dies, that doesn't mean the child is necessarily at risk. You would hope that Social Services wouldn't be called, because relatives would be there and they'd be tekking the child. If there's nobody in the house and the neighbour rings the police and says, 'This 4-year-old is next door and his mum (or grandma's) died', Social Services will come in and do whatever it is they have to do. So there needs to be a plan in place, something written down. There needs to be another family member that knows – and then the group could continue to support anyone else who's looking after the children. An auntie or uncle could join the group.

Apart from this, grandparents or other carers face so many issues. Finance is a major one and the time that they have to give to the child, the problems that these children bring with behaviour, their own children – still using perhaps. And of course health, and social isolation – no social life whatsoever. You can't plan anything for yourself (even a quiet walk in the park); instead you have to stand there pushing someone on the swing! And being out of touch with the school system, fashions, social media. Not understanding new parenting skills about child development. And always wondering, 'Am I doing the right thing?' For normal grandparents it's all very well and good to tell their children how to bring up their kids, but they can walk away. For us, it's still a learning curve, just like it was first time round – and it's harder, because you're older.

The good thing about working at Bridge: they've always let me get on with it. I do have to report back to my managers and I think they are interested – they can put it in their AGM [Annual General Meeting] annual report that this is happening. The carers' service is a little service in a massive service and it doesn't get much recognition. The drug *users* who are committing crimes are going to get more funding and more workers than the carers. But they've left me completely to get on with it – they knew how passionate I was. They didn't have any worry that instead of me doing something I was nipping off to the gym.

Campaigning for Grandparents

We did some campaigning for grandparents too. I heard from the Family Rights Group that there was going to be a rally in London set up by Grandparents Plus. They said, 'We will pay the train fare and supply refreshments, and all the children would have a free go on the London Eye.' So I asked the grandparents if they wanted to attend, and they said, 'Lovely'. The reason behind it was lobbying Westminster to speak to all the MPs, about the issues of bringing up grandchildren, and not getting support or finance and so on. We all had red T-shirts with 'Grandparents for Grandchildren' on them. Getting there was absolutely so stressful for me. Getting on the train to go to London was fine – I'd bought a lot of colouring books and crayons, and the children all coloured together. They drew me pictures, which I've saved – 'Thank you Mary', some of 'em put – lovely pictures. They all got on very well. And then when we got to London it was tubes. That scared me – because imagine, losing a grandparent or a grandchild on the platform if the doors shut! Leaving someone behind. We didn't all have mobiles – I mean, when was it we went there – 2009? And some of the grandparents had never been to London.

When we got to the meeting in Westminster they had a play area for the children. There was a big screen with statistics that told you how many grandchildren are cared for by grandparents in this country – I should imagine that Families First and Grandparents Plus had done this. There were lots of different speakers – Grandparents Plus and Family Rights Group and MPs. Then there were questions from the audience, and I stood up and said, 'Foster carers are paid a substantial amount, which is brilliant, but why can't grandparents get a similar payment?' And a minister said, 'Well that would open t'floodgates.' I said, 'Floodgates to what?' I said, 'Any benefit opens floodgates, why should this be any different?'

So it was very good, there were so many there! Maybe 300–400. It was for grandparents looking after their grandchildren full-time, and the majority was because of substance abuse and mental health problems. There wasn't the media coverage that everyone probably hoped for. But there was a magazine printed by Grandparents Plus with a picture of all of us at the event on the front.

It didn't really get us anywhere, when I think about it, but you've got to plod on with these things – there's been others. Me and the grandparents went to a conference in Pudsey Civic Hall, which was run by Grandparents Plus. It was addressed by Nigel Priestley, who is a solicitor campaigning for grandparents, and an MP was there – Greg Mulholland I think. There were several different ones that we went to. Every time I heard anything, we went to it. We had a joint meeting with the grandparents in Liverpool, to see how far they'd got with campaigning. They'd been running a lot longer, and we were asking them what they'd been doing, which at the time was quite helpful.

After we met at the conference I asked Nigel Priestley, 'Could you come and meet our group?' He met the group and was really good. He told them about their rights. He told them about Care Orders and Residence Orders and Special Guardianship. He explained to them that if you've got a Residency Order, the Local Authorities have got no obligation to you whatsoever; however, if you haven't, then they have got a duty to help. And that's where he can help. He was so knowledgeable.

If we want to do campaigning I need to put it by my manager. Say, 'This is what the Grandparents' Group is wanting to do.' And then he would tek it to the overall management team. And I think the only thing they would probably say is, in certain cases, 'If the media's gonna be there, we definitely don't want you to use Bridge's name.' Depending what it is, I'd ask 'em, 'Could you just tell me why, so that I can explain to the group?' And I'd have to say to 'em, 'Well, can I be part of that?' And they might say, 'Well you can, but it would have to be in your own time. Or you could do it in Bridge time, but again, you know – you're supporting them, but not to bring us into it.' But so far they haven't objected.

The Professional and the Personal

I have had quite a lot of ill-health (two heart attacks and an abscess on my lung), and then my son died and I was off for 6 weeks. When I was ill, no one took over the service – it was kind of just left. But the groups went on running. They are quite capable – I mean, a lot of the time, there's no need for me to sit in. A group will never be lost, because they've got each other.

My son was a heroin user for 17 years. Then he stopped using, which was excellent, but he started drinking instead. And 3 years later, tragically he was dead from alcohol misuse. I don't have my grandchildren, and when I set up The Grandparents Group all them years ago I never thought it would happen to me. Parents sometimes have to live with the fact that their sons and daughters are substance misusers.

Others may be paedophiles or decide to rob banks! It's easy for us to blame ourselves, but nobody out there has got the right to judge anybody. And our children made a choice – a bad choice. As an adult everybody has a choice.

I was devastated when I had to face redundancy. My job is jointly funded by Bradford Council and government, and the funding for drugs work has been cut, but it came out of the blue. I went to a meeting with the Council and I said, 'I just want to know where my clients are going to go, that's a real concern of mine.' I was told, 'We'd have to look at that' – nobody's looked at it *first*! There was talk of it being cut to a part-time job, with a lot less salary and no guarantees. I love the job, but I can't afford to work on these terms. It will be heartbreaking for me to leave, but I think The Grandparents Group is very well established and they will still be able to meet at Bridge.

Carers don't commit crimes or hang from Big Ben, so it's hard to get recognised nationally. They talk about families and carers in parliament, but really, the drug users (who are committing crimes) are going to get more funding and therefore more drug workers – so the carers' service is gonna be the first to go, which has proved correct.

The grandchildren are our future, and I think that children have got a better chance if the grandparents step in, than the ones who don't and go into care. That child, for whatever reason their parents have misused substances – they've got a right to live a normal life. It's not about the drug users, it's not about the grandparents, it's about the children. Most grandparents would never dream of giving up this part of their life so that the grandchildren can have a better future. The love of grandparents in the group, and all the thousands more grandparents doing this is amazing.

Afterword

Grandparenting in Challenging Circumstances: Understanding the Impact of Early Childhood Trauma on Development and Well-being

Caroline Archer

Caroline Archer is an adoptive parent of four children, a grandparent and great-grandparent, and a writer on attachment, trauma and adoption. Through her own experiences of parenting, and through education, training and practice over more than two decades, she has gained valuable insights into the behaviours many adoptive children display owing to their early experiences. Abandonment, neglect and abuse have a traumatic impact on youngsters' attachment and development. Caroline has worked extensively with adopters and practitioners in adoption and in the support of children and families. This work has informed her involvement in developing effective therapeutic strategies using a neuro-developmental approach that encompasses the interactions between mind, body and brain. Such strategies help parents and caregivers make sense of, and manage, the potentially long-term consequences of early adverse experiences on their children's physical, emotional, social, educational and psychological well-being. Her work has been disseminated in several publications.

* * *

The candid life stories in this book are very familiar. As an adoptive parent and grandparent, I identify with the Yorkshire grandparents' struggles to make sense of their adult children's ongoing difficulties, and understand and meet their grandchildren's needs. I came to adoption believing that 'love would be enough'. Gradually I learnt that even the youngest children placed in adoptive families carry with them 'hidden hurts' that affect their physical, emotional, social and intellectual development throughout their lives. Some of our adoptive children came into our families as babies; others were pre-schoolers or of school age; some were accompanied by siblings; some are known to have been exposed to alcohol and/or harmful drugs. Some had spent time on neonatal intensive care wards, often unaccompanied. Some suffered extended periods in hospital, with chronic pain or painful clinical interventions. Hence all of our adoptive children were exposed to some degree of early adversity and, in consequence, to the toxic neurohormones associated with separation, inconsistent care, frequent changes of carer, pain, neglect and abuse. Their behaviour reflected the traumatic impact of these early adverse experiences.

Early Trauma

Traumatic challenges to the body, brain and mind can begin in the womb, with exposure of the foetus to harmful substances, such as alcohol and drugs, and the influence of toxic stress hormones shared through the umbilical cord with their mothers. The overproduction of these neurohormones can be triggered by seemingly innocuous events such as a parent's craving for cigarettes. Far greater are the effects, for unborn infants, when 'hit' by the harmful chemical compounds within alcohol and mood-altering or pain-relieving drugs (parentally induced 'stress hits'). Adverse levels of foetal stress can also be induced by parental fears of physical or verbal assault from partners, threats from dealers, the constant anxiety of avoiding detection by police and Social Services or the lack of money to support their dependency. Whilst all healthy adults experience some stress, they possess the capacity to process occasional challenges to their bodies' stress management systems. Chronic substance use and chronic stress gradually overwhelm these natural restorative processes.

Unborn infants are not only physically ill-equipped to manage exposure to stress; also their brain and nervous system development is seriously compromised by high or chronic levels of stress neurohormones, particularly cortisol. Consequently they may demonstrate many of the emotional, behavioural and cognitive difficulties associated with attention deficit disorders, autistic spectrum disorders, foetal alcohol spectrum disorders and/or attachment disorders. Exposure to early adverse experiences can both affect the 'communication pathways' by which the body and brain share information, and alter the structure of specific brain areas. If these changes are not appropriately identified and managed at an early stage they can persist throughout childhood and into adulthood, preventing children from reaching their potential.

As an adopter and an active participant in an adoptive grandparents' support group, I have become increasingly aware of how these difficulties – the consequences of developmental attachment trauma – can be passed to the next generation. Our adoptive Grandparents Group, like the Yorkshire grandparents, are predominantly women experiencing serious concerns about their daughters' children. Contact with the children of our sons is often more tenuous, being dependent on current relationships with sons' partners. We are not all raising these children full-time; more often we are drawn into a pattern of 'revolving-door' care, taking our grandchildren into our homes for days or weeks, without warning or agreed terms, at the behest of our adult children.

Fight, Flight and Freeze

Over time, typical patterns of behaviour became evident in our adopted children, which echo the descriptions of grandchildren from the Yorkshire group. The most frequently reported cluster of challenges come from 'acting-out' behaviours such as tantrums, hyperactivity, sleep or eating problems, lack of cooperation, impulsivity, destructiveness or aggression. Difficulties at school often co-exist. It is hard for caregivers to make sense of these behaviours, let alone find effective ways of handling them. As children grow, these issues can become more challenging and leave caregivers feeling exhausted and isolated. They may receive conflicting advice from parents, family members, friends, health visitors, GPs, schools and Child and Adolescent Mental Health Services (CAMHS). Stress levels rise and they feel increasingly frustrated, angry, inadequate and shame-filled.

What Do We Mean by Trauma?

In simple terms, trauma is an injury to mind or body which calls out for healing (Waites 1993). It is an individual's *subjective* perceptions of events as terrifying, overwhelming their capacity to cope and threatening 'life, bodily integrity or sanity' (Pearlman and Saakvitne 1995, p.60) that define them as traumatic. Whilst the physical wounds of abuse, accident or injury may be visible, wounds to the mind remain hidden – evident only in the distressed and distressing behaviours of traumatised individuals. There are neurobiological changes to the brain and neural circuitry that underpin such behaviours, and the route to recovery ('repair') becomes increasingly arduous the longer that identification and intervention are delayed.

The adverse effects of single, major distressing events and ongoing, or intermittent, chronic adverse experiences are widely known. Specific trauma-related neurohormones, such as adrenalin and cortisol, have been identified, and their effects on the body and brain explored. It is recognised that having secure attachments and community supports can be powerful protectors against the traumatic, overwhelming feelings of fear, abandonment and helplessness in threatening situations that lead to the long-term adverse effects identified as post-traumatic stress disorder. Adults who experienced consistent, responsive parenting and have established mature social relationships are less likely to suffer post-traumatic stress. They possess the social resources, the capacity to reflect on and make sense of their experiences and the resilience to 'bounce back'.

The recognition of developmental trauma, differentially affecting children, is more recent. Infants and young children experiencing traumatic events, such as the disruptions of famine and war, or exposure to mood-altering drugs (including alcohol), neglect or abuse, lack these protective factors. Their attachments are still being established or consolidated and they are developmentally immature – hence their brains and nervous systems are highly vulnerable to being 'flooded' by traumatic stress neurohormones. Even brief experiences of 'being alone and scared', which may have little lasting effect on an adult, can be overwhelming to babies and young children. Moments can feel like 'forever' and subjectively experienced as life-threatening – permanently affecting youngsters' perceptions of themselves, their safety and their world. Their bodies and minds become 'primed' to anticipate and respond to danger, resulting in either hypervigilance, hyperreactivity and non-compliance ('acting out'), or timidity, hypo-reactivity, submissiveness or 'shut down' ('acting in'). Children's behaviour can swing from one pattern to another according to circumstance (Archer and Gordon 2013; Lyons 2017).

Van der Kolk (2005) and D'Andrea et al. (2012) propose the introduction of a new term that recognises the unique effects of developmental trauma on the well-being of children and young people. Developmental trauma disorder provides an inclusive diagnosis embracing many of the symptoms currently used to define and delineate attention deficit disorders, attachment disorders, conduct and oppositional defiant disorders and autistic spectrum disorders.

In doing so it points the way towards focused, neurodevelopmentally based therapies designed to understand and heal (Perry 2009; van der Kolk 2014; Levy and Orlans 2014; Lyons 2017), rather than contain and manage children's behaviour – the 'language' through which they express their (dis)stress (Archer and Gordon 2012).

A much less obvious but 'more comfortable' pattern of behaviours can be described as 'acting in'. Here, children may be quiet, helpful, cooperative, responsible, submissive, eager to please, affectionate and caring towards siblings and others. They tend to 'think of others not themselves'. Their need for closeness, encouragement and reassurance is endearing to caregivers and teachers alike. Yet the basis of these 'pro-social' behaviours is not security and growing maturity but fear: of separation and loss, of being hurt emotionally or physically, of never being 'good enough', of the unknown (Archer 2015). They fear being 'found out': that others will see them as they see themselves – unlovable. When, occasionally but inevitably, they 'melt down' or are 'naughty', this confirms their belief that they are intrinsically 'bad' and must try ever harder to be 'good': an impossible and highly stressful challenge for children. As they approach adolescence their ability to cope with such high levels of stress can lead to mental health issues and/or provoke 'acting-out' behaviours.

As adoptive parents, we readily identified and struggled with our 'fight-or-flight' kids. Few of us realised the significance of their 'freeze' behaviours, at least until they hit the teenage years. It was our 'acting-out' children who created tensions within the family – their frustrated and angry responses often resonating with our own. We frequently felt we were failing our children and were ashamed of our own negative feelings, the reactions of our family and friends, and those of our children's friends and families. Like the Yorkshire grandparents we often felt isolated and judged; the conflicting advice we received further increased our sense of confusion and powerlessness. On the other hand, we delighted in our 'acting-in' children's willingness to comply, their helpfulness, their self-help skills, their popularity and their eagerness to learn; we accepted their quietness, 'shyness' and need to be close as endearing and rewarding. We reacted with shock to 'meltdowns', unwittingly increasing their shame and reinforcing their struggle to be 'good' at all costs.

These two contrasting patterns of behaviour are best understood as opposite sides of the same coin. They are survival responses, resulting from early traumatic experiences, based on identical fears but following alternative neurodevelopmental pathways: 'fight or flight' ('blowing up', 'acting out'), or 'freeze' ('shutting down', 'acting in').

Substance Misuse and 'Good-Enough' Parenting

Infants have no inbuilt 'self-soothing' strategies; they acquire neurobiological self-regulation through shared interactions with their parent(s). This forms the basis of their attachment and development. Most parental figures pass on these self-regulatory patterns to their children through repeated and consistent interactions with them. They download their 'rebalancing software' to their children, helping them feel calm, comforted, secure and able to trust the world around them. Over time their youngsters become more proficient in regulating ('rebalancing') their own responses and feelings, and gain self-awareness, self-control and self-confidence.

They become increasingly able to think things through – to negotiate challenges, manage their fears and move out into the world. This is unlikely to be the case for substance-using parents.

Substance use itself can be understood as one of several patterns of acquired self-soothing and fear management adopted by adults exposed to early or later trauma. It often begins as an unconscious attempt to self-regulate, through self-medication, to numb emotional pain and blank out the threatening world. Besides early attachment and developmental trauma, it is important to note that genetics, pre-existing mental health issues, loss of significant family members and a challenging social environment may also be pre-disposing factors. For example, loss of a sibling to addiction (as in Chapter 3), peer pressure or widespread use of drugs or alcohol within the local community can make young people vulnerable to 'experimenting' with addictive substances. It may not take long before the need becomes physiological, because of the establishment of 'reward pathways' in the brain. Increased tolerance soon leads to increased demand, as the user attempts to re-regulate. Significantly, the earlier drug use begins, the more likely it is to become problematic, since adolescent brains undergo developmental changes as dramatic as those of infancy.

Substance users demonstrate limited self-care and social skills and lack 'emotional literacy'; they will therefore be less capable of meeting the 'feeding and watering' needs (Gordon 2015) of their children, let alone being 'emotionally available' to them. Their primary focus is on attempting to manage their own needs and feelings: funding their addiction, maintaining relationships with volatile partners, or avoiding threats from dealers, arrest by the police or intervention from children's safeguarding services. They may prioritise acquiring high-tech electronic equipment, computer games or the latest smartphone over attending to their children's needs – often in an attempt to feel better about themselves.

This style of parenting is as much a pattern of abuse and/or neglect as physical or sexual violence towards children, and should be recognised and responded to in the same way. Appropriate interventions should be provided not only in the short term but also throughout children's journeys through childhood and adolescence to adulthood. It should be recognised that caring for children traumatised in this way demands special parenting skills – information about which may not be readily available within the local community. The accounts in this book demonstrate that awareness and recognition of the direct effects on developing infants of exposure to toxic substances is still lacking within many children's social, educational and mental health services. In Chapter 7 we see that concern about foetal alcohol spectrum disorder (FASD) was not raised until a third child reached toddlerhood, although the two elder siblings clearly displayed many of the behavioural problems associated with it. Nor are the effects on the capacity to provide 'good-enough' parenting by substance-using parents adequately recognised.

Reparenting Traumatised Children

With growing understanding of the causes of, and reasons for, traumatised children's behaviours, we can find ways of altering them. An awareness of the link between trauma, attachment and development and the concept of behaviour as 'children's first language' (Archer and Gordon 2013) allows us to create more effective responses. Rather than using cognitive behavioural approaches to help our 'acting-out' children 'behave' or 'act their age' – using reasoned discussions and sanctions – we can identify their intense fears and understand their hyperreactivity in terms of poor self-regulation. They remain vulnerable to intense, unmodulated sensations and emotions, and were therefore responding as infants or toddlers – although they might appear, moments later, to be in total control. In the former behaviour they are acting according to their 'developmental' or 'emotional' age; in the latter according to their 'chronological age'.

Children exposed to early adversity benefit from 'bottom-up' reparenting, to fill in their 'developmental gaps', rather than 'top-down' approaches that assume they have acquired the skills to 'think before they act'. Both 'acting-out' and 'acting-in' children benefit from this therapeutic reparenting approach. When children experience security and co-regulation from consistent parental figures, allowing these normal developmental attachment sequences to take place, they are then able to feel, play, learn and think about themselves, others and the world in mature, reasoning ways. If caregivers respond to 'tantrums' calmly, remaining with and co-regulating them, traumatised children can begin to learn to manage their own distress and to trust in others and themselves. Conversely, 'time-outs' or 'thinking time' increase trauma-reactive children's fear of abandonment and raise their stress levels. 'Meaningful discussions' go over children's heads until they experience safety and co-regulation from calm, available caregivers, who can help them re-regulate.

'Acting in' children benefit from self-regulating parents who can actively encourage them, through modelling and joining in, to be playful, 'silly', 'naughty' or 'loud', without 'losing it'. This allows children to practise 'letting go' whilst not feeling 'out of control', and to learn to 'feel OK' and that 'the world doesn't end' if they don't keep their heads, and their feelings, down.

Trauma-based behavioural challenges are evident in the Yorkshire grandparents' accounts of their grandchildren, and the parenting difficulties these grandparents face remain disconcertingly similar to ours. Yet it appears that the awareness, education and support that are becoming more widespread within adoption and fostering services have not reached parallel support services for families of substance-using parents. It is important that the traumatic commonalities underpinning the issues of adopted children and those of substance-using parents and their offspring are acknowledged. Identifying the traumatic early developmental experiences that impact on children's attachment and development, and hence their global well-being, should be at the forefront of service providers' minds – be it doctors, teachers, social workers, community workers, psychologists or therapists – when seeking to support these vulnerable children. Recent initiatives by UK Public Health bodies (e.g. GIG/NHS Iechyd Cyhoeddus Cymru Public Health Wales 2015) are beginning both to assess 'adverse childhood experiences' (ACEs) as measures of impact on families' and children's health and well-being, and to inform early identification and intervention.

As future best practice, it is to be hoped that this will include recognition of the valuable contribution that grandparents provide. We have seen that grandparents often play a pivotal role as caregivers: they are the 'first responders', society's 'front line' and their grandchildren's lifeline. Whilst it is challenging to manage traumatised children's behaviours, and 'success' is not always palpable, grandparents' commitment to providing stability and love is invaluable. Grandparents need to feel acknowledged and informed (with adequate resources including financial, respite, health and emotional supports) to enable them to sustain the level of care their grandchildren need and deserve.

Between a Rock and a Hard Place

The turmoil of emotionally conflicting loyalties to adult children and grandchildren, and the sense of diminishing strength that comes with age, are themes common to both groups of grandparents. First, grandparents are 'between a rock and a hard place' – often from the moment they become aware their daughter (or son) is expecting a child, and certainly once the child is born. Their adult children's troubled behaviour has often been evident over many years, and relationships are frequently strained. Grandparents have generally experienced serious concerns about their adult children's behaviour from their teenage years, including substance use, aggression, unpredictability, petty offending, lack of respect for authority, manipulation, 'reformulating the truth', 'borrowing', promiscuity, poor personal care and chaotic lifestyles. Serious mental health issues may have become increasingly evident over time. Hence the arrival of a child can weigh heavily from day one. Where difficulties were previously less evident, the challenges to their adult children of managing relationships with partners, budgeting and taking care of a vulnerable child or children may cause the veneer to crack.

Grandparents normally anticipate the arrival of grandchildren with visions of happy, playful times. They look forward to 'having the best bits' of their grandchildren, then returning them home and continuing their busy lives and/or equally busy relaxation. Babysitting and child care, with adult children returning to work, is negotiated, and financial support offered within acceptable limits. Such is not the case for grandparents with troubled adult children. Demands for child care are often at little or no notice and for unspecified periods. Grandchildren may be 'dumped' when their mothers feel they cannot cope, are 'too tired', need 'to go out for a bit', go to the pub or get a 'fix'.

For grandparents it can become an unenviable choice between keeping firm boundaries or stepping in, fearing that their grandchildren will be left alone at home. The 'rescued' grandchildren may be inadequately clothed, hungry or dirty, distressed, confused, demanding or clingy. They will often ask, 'When is Mummy coming?' or 'When am I going home?' Such upsetting questions themselves pose difficulties. Whether to provide a 'cover story' – placating a child with 'In a while' or 'When Mummy's better' – or be more open? How and when to acknowledge grandchildren's feelings of hurt, anxiety, abandonment and self-blame ('If I hadn't spilled my milk Mum wouldn't have got angry' or 'If I'd just been kinder to Mum she'd have stayed at home')? Similar dilemmas occur when grandparents are asked directly for money. Should they make funds available in the desperate hope that the money will be used appropriately to feed or clothe the child, or risk facing accusatory or aggressive reactions if they decline? Will this anger be taken out on their grandchildren? Will their financial assistance be supporting their adult children's habit? Should they draw a line in the sand? If so, when and how?

Grandparents are often 'the immoveable rocks' when they find themselves in these 'hard places'. They often put their own plans and feelings on hold to meet the immediate demands of their adult children and, simultaneously, of their grandchildren. They may wonder what they themselves did wrong that their children act in such irresponsible and seemingly uncaring ways, when these are in fact the results of substance use. Just as grandparents accept their new caring role, their adult children may turn up to collect their offspring, sometimes without a word of acknowledgement. If grandparents question their daughters' or sons' actions, some face responses like 'You only care about your grandchildren, you never care(d) about me.' In such situations, with feelings running high, grandparents risk being accused by their adult children of 'kidnap', or of being abusive themselves. Typically, bad feelings continue until the next time help is needed, when such difficulties are 'forgotten'. Their adult children can appear oblivious to their vulnerable, often-distressed offspring stuck in the middle, whose care and well-being should be paramount. Acutely aware of this, grandparents may avoid challenging their children so as to minimise their grandchildren's exposure to conflict.

Grandparents with troubled adult children may fear openly acknowledging their distressing experiences at home to their grandchildren, knowing that an unwitting comment later to Mum, like 'Nanny says you're.../you don't...', could strain relationships further. Yet avoiding the issue can feel to the grandchildren like denial of their experience and feelings. Perceived (or actual) challenges to adult children's parenting capability or standing occur, too, when grandparents make comments about the state of their children's homes, their management of money or their behaviour. Similar responses can be generated by concerns expressed about the cleanliness of grandchildren, their lack of routine, their diet, their inconsistent attendance at nursery or school, their behaviour or how they are disciplined.

Grandparents can feel used and abused when they are, in fact, attempting to improve their grandchildren's care. We should not underestimate the contradictory pressures they face. It is little wonder that they often feel inadequate, confused or humiliated, lose self-confidence and develop a sense of impotence. In such intolerable situations they may experience an undercurrent of anger towards their adult children as they watch their grandchildren's distress. They begin to question their own parenting capacities, past and present, and may feel they are being too judgemental or insufficiently supportive. They come to feel responsible for creating or resolving the whole desperate situation, yet have little control over it. Like abused partners they may assume the blame and shame that is so paralysing. This in turn makes them less likely to share their concerns and desperation with family or friends, whom they fear will judge them badly or will not understand, particularly if they sense the frustration and anger grandparents are struggling to contain. They may play down the situation to protect themselves, or their family and friends, from further distress. Their isolation becomes ever greater.

Getting Help

Perhaps one of the most difficult dilemmas grandparents face is in deciding if, when or how to approach the authorities with concerns about their adult children and grandchildren. As the narratives in this book recount, approaches to medical or mental health services to provide or obtain essential information are often met with concerns over confidentiality and/or requests to obtain permission from their adult children before information can be shared. Yet often adult children are unaware of, unable to deal with or in denial that they are experiencing significant difficulties. Since parent–adult-children relationships are often precarious, they can worsen if these issues are raised.

Grandparents may feel they should prioritise their vulnerable grandchildren's well-being by alerting health visitors, nursery workers or social workers, yet wonder whether it would be better to compromise and remain silent, leaving them room to continue 'holding' and supporting their adult children and grandchildren on a day-to-day basis. Although they may wish to discuss their worries about their adult children's capacity to manage areas of their lives, such as budgeting or holding down a tenancy, their transient lifestyle, potentially dangerous behaviour or volatile mental state, grandparents can have understandable fears that involving relevant authorities could have devastating effects on family relationships and may lead to children being taken into care. They can feel disloyal to their adult children, or fear that accusations of disloyalty might trigger a violent backlash from them. Such souring of fragile relationships can lead to withdrawal of contact between grandparents and grandchildren for lengthy periods – a painful and destabilising loss for all parties.

The painful decision to pass on significant information to the authorities is done with trepidation regarding the outcome for their families. Social Services may question why they have not spoken out sooner, if the issues are long-standing, or indeed their current motives for doing so. Corroborating evidence may be required but not readily available. After visiting the adult children's homes, the situation may be deemed tolerable or warranting only a watching brief. The responsibility for protecting vulnerable grandchildren then continues to sit heavily on grandparents' shoulders, alongside a growing sense of guilt, impotence and inadequacy.

Information provided by grandparents, which they believe to have been given in confidence, may be passed on to their adult children by social workers during investigations or case conferences. This can further destabilise fragile relationships between adult children and their parents – with serious repercussions for the grandchildren's well-being. Whilst striving for transparency and trust in their dealings with families, and to act in the children's best interests, practitioners should hold in mind that grandparents may be unaware of the limits of confidentiality when divulging intimate information about their adult children's behaviour and emotional states. In seeking to safeguard these vulnerable children they should consider the potentially destructive intra-familial dynamics that may come into play.

The stressful experiences of grandparents when a formal safeguarding decision is made are powerfully underlined in several chapters of this book. Despite being only too aware of the months or years of inappropriate, inadequate or unpredictable care of their grandchildren, it still comes as a bombshell when a decision for their removal is taken. Requests for grandparents to become their grandchildren's carers often come at short notice and with little clarity about their future status as carers or the duration of the placement. There are numerous examples in the individual accounts of the distress and confusion this generates in grandparents, both directly, as their lives are put on hold, and indirectly through their grandchildren's distress and need for explanations and reassurance.

In our adoptive Grandparents Group this has occurred less often, though sometimes removal of grandchildren from their parents' care has been followed by a decision to place them for adoption outside the family. This is experienced by grandparents as a second extremely painful loss, since contact with grandchildren is frequently terminated or seriously restricted. Long-standing grief over the loss of the child they envisaged in adulthood is echoed in the shattering of dreams for their grandchildren. Handling any limited, permitted contact, whether by 'letterbox', telephone or face to face, brings further distress – a situation beyond the experience of most. Questions arise about what to say in letters or calls, or where and when to visit. Grandparents experience uncertainty as to their role, or even what to call themselves during contact. If their adult children are not granted contact, or handle it inappropriately, this can further affect relationships between grandparents and their adult children.

The adoptive grandparents in our group are predominantly caring for grandchildren 'at a distance', with adult children retaining primary responsibility. This, combined with periods of 'revolving-door' full-time care, may continue indefinitely. The well-being of the grandchildren is primarily dependent on their parents, who may continue to be uncooperative, unreliable, unpredictable, neglectful and/or abusive. Grandparents' ability to intervene actively is limited by their adult children's legal status as parents and their willingness to accept appropriate help and support on grandparents' terms. Their emotional instability and continuing neediness, due to their own early traumatic experiences of hurt and loss, limits their capacity to sustain parenting responsibility or put their children's needs first. The difficult challenges shared by the adoptive grandparents and the Yorkshire group are likely to remain ongoing, or increase as years pass, but a desperate need for more understanding and sensitive support is evident.

Losses and Gains

Experiences of hurt, grief and loss across all three generations are clear. Grandparents may feel overwhelmed by a strong sense of responsibility to their adult children and their grandchildren, becoming heavier over the years and accompanied by an increasing, and potentially paralysing, sense of loss of control over their own lives. They may long for the easy mutual dependence and independence that timely emancipation from the nuclear family brings, made increasingly potent as they watch the lives and family relationships of friends and colleagues blossoming and changing over time.

The losses of the substance-using adult children can be equally painful. Separation from their parents may have been premature, before they were ready, psychologically and socially, and when their 'top-down' thought processes were still overruled by powerful, emotionally driven responses. In some cases, there will have been actual loss of a parent or significant member of their family: through illness and death or through an ongoing absence in their lives. Subsequently, as their behaviour and/or mental health deteriorate, they are likely to lose the support of, and/or contact with, at least some family members. They may lose friendships, jobs, accommodation and status within the community. There may be serious loss of health, self-respect, life prospects and sense of control over their lives. Most painful of all is likely to be the loss of their children, whether temporarily or permanently. They fear the loss of their children's love and respect. Sometimes the pain of such losses is turned into anger directed at their parents, whom they may perceive as usurping their own role as caregivers.

For grandchildren raised by grandparents and for adoptees there is a deep loss, or 'primal wound' (Verrier 1994), when the uniquely intimate bond between mother and baby or young child is broken. However, whilst the physical bond is broken, the metaphorical 'umbilic bond' persists. The apparent gain of a loving adoptive family or of grandparents stepping in is counterbalanced by separation from, and loss of, the birth parent. Their primal connection retains its power. At one level the grandchildren 'know' that they are loved and protected by their new caregivers, yet on the other hand the wish for an idealised reunion with their birth parent(s) remains palpable. Lacking a gradual, positive experience at the normal separation stage of toddlerhood, such children find the parallel process of separation challenging as they approach adulthood. A tendency towards premature emancipation provides an added dynamic of loss, and sense of abandonment, whether or not they have actively brought about this separation from their family home.

All of the grandchildren have suffered early attachment trauma, where exposure to toxic substances in utero, neglect, abuse, separations or losses disrupts neurobiological development, with potentially life-long effects. This represents failure to thrive in a global developmental context and the potential losses to children are enormous. For these children, the loss of a healthy start in life threatens their childhood. They lose the parental nurture they deserve, experiencing instead unpredictability, rejection and hurt. They may blame themselves for their circumstances, lack of sensori-motor regulation and integration, poor emotional awareness and regulation, psychological difficulties, poor social skills, weak executive functioning and limited educational achievement. Cognitive processes such as reasoning, the ability to negotiate or compromise and self-organisation remain immature. Early adversity can also make children more difficult to (re)parent, due to its effects on their bodies, brains and minds (including their ability to trust) creating additional challenges in already vulnerable situations. Thus, traumatised children stand to lose their place and way in the world, losing connections to themselves and to their community.

Whilst moving in with caring grandparents appears to bring only positives, as with adoption it is often accompanied by powerful, conflicting feelings. Children's responses are complex. Moving out of their birth family home to live with grandparents – be it through 'the revolving door', or more permanently, informally or formally – is experienced as both gain and loss. Youngsters may welcome the calmer, more predictable, more comfortable home environment within which they find themselves, but, as for adoptees, there is a simultaneous, pervasive sense of loss. However distressing their experiences whilst living with their birth family, it represents 'home': the unique space they shared with their parent(s) and to whom they felt uniquely connected from their conception.

During adolescence, as they experience more independence, children may actively seek to be reunited with birth parents. This may mean vehemently rejecting the grandparents who have been their main caretakers for years (e.g. Chapter 5), creating a further painful loss of their grandparents' day-by-day support, as well as loss of friends, school and community networks. Grandparents, too, are likely to feel hurt by their rejection. They experience the loss of the close relationship they experienced with the grandchildren who had become so much part of their daily lives.

It Takes a Community to Raise a Child

One of society's primal and primary roles is to provide support networks for the benefit of its members 'from cradle to grave'. In evolutionary terms, society facilitates the survival of the species. Part of this role is to create safe space and support for the essential task of bringing vulnerable newborns and youngsters to maturity. This is particularly evident in 'higher mammals', where the gestation and development of offspring are prolonged. Rarely do individuals raise the next generation alone. How much more vital is the support of the community when additional challenges exist – where parents are older, or in poor health or are caring for less-healthy children? For grandparents of troubled adult children caring for their grandchildren directly or indirectly, many or all of these factors come into play. Yet they frequently feel unsupported and ill-informed, with their needs, and those of their adult children, poorly understood. An increasingly sophisticated awareness of the long-term effects of early adversity (ACEs) on every aspect of children's development must be fostered in all agencies and shared with the struggling families they support.

Finally, the invaluable role that support groups can play for grandparents shouldering the challenging task of reparenting traumatised children must be recognised. The commitment, wisdom and experience that grandparents bring to such groups should not be underestimated. Groups can provide mutual support, helping grandparents feel less alone, increasing their understanding of the issues they face, bolstering their confidence and strengthening their resilience. They can enable grandparents to value themselves, accept their limitations, develop realistic expectations about what they can and cannot achieve, and recognise that even 'minor' successes should be celebrated.

References

Archer, C. (2015) 'Smile Though Your Heart is Aching: Therapeutic Parent Mentoring for "Good Kids" and Their Families.' In C. Archer, C. Drury and J. Hills (eds) *Healing the Hidden Hurts*. London: Jessica Kingsley Publishers.

Archer, C. and Gordon, G. (2012) *Reparenting the Child Who Hurts*. London: Jessica Kingsley Publishers.

D'Andrea, W., Ford, J., Stolbach, B., Spinazzola, J. and van der Kolk, B.A. (2012) 'Understanding interpersonal trauma in children: Why we need a developmentally appropriate trauma diagnosis.' *American Journal of Orthopsychiatry 82*, 2, 187–200.

GIG/NHS Iechyd Cyhoeddus Cymru/Public Health Wales (2015) *Welsh Adverse Experiences (ACE) Study*. Bellis, M.A., Ashton, K., Hughes, K., Bishop J. and Paranjothy, S. Cardiff, UK: PH Wales NHS Trust.

Gordon, C. (2015) 'Beyond Feeding and Watering: Trauma and Attachment-based Court Assessments.' In C. Archer, C. Drury and J. Hills (eds) *Healing the Hidden Hurts*. London: Jessica Kingsley Publishers.

Levy, T. and Orlans, M. (2014) *Attachment, Trauma and Healing* (second edition). London: Jessica Kingsley Publishers.

Lyons, S. (2017) *The Repair of Early Trauma: A 'Bottom Up' Approach*. Accessed on 20/02/18 at http://beaconhouse.org.uk/developmental trauma/the-repair-of-early-trauma.

Pearlman, L.A. and Saakvitne K.W. (1995) *Trauma and Transference and the Therapist: Countertransference in Psychotherapy with Incest Survivors.* New York: Norton.

Perry, B.D. (2009) 'Examining child maltreatment through a neuro-developmental lens: Clinical applications of the neurosequential model of therapeutics.' *Journal of Loss and Trauma 14,* 240–255.

van der Kolk, B.A. (2005) 'Developmental trauma disorder: Towards a rational diagnosis for children with complex traumatic histories.' *Psychiatric Annals 35,* 401–408.

van der Kolk, B.A. (2014) *The Body Keeps the Score: Brain, Mind, and Body in the Healing of Trauma*: New York: Penguin Group.

Verrier, N. (1994) *The Primal Wound.* Baltimore, MD: Gateway.

Waites, E. (1993) *Trauma and Survival.* New York: Norton and Co.

Postscript

As grandparents, our steadfastness and determination to hold onto our grandchildren is constantly tested, but we are still here. Most of our grandchildren are displaying extreme 'acting-out' behaviours as they reach adolescence, with two of them putting themselves in dangerous situations. More positively, one of our grandchildren is now at university and two are in college. The majority have transitioned to secondary schools where they are coping, even whilst we find that support for, and recognition of, their difficulties is often poorer than at primary schools. We have received more medical and therapeutic help but little of it has been very effective. Our adult children who survive are still struggling with the legacy of drug and alcohol addictions and remain a responsibility.

We are not professionals and we do not claim to have perfect solutions to the challenges we have been forced to confront in caring for our traumatised grandchildren. Where it was accessible, we have listened and adapted professional advice to our individual situations. We have also devised our own creative approaches as best we can, recognising that our previous parenting experience was invaluable but did not give us enough preparation for such an undertaking. More than anything we have looked to each other in The Grandparents Group for understanding and comfort in adversity and for support in our resolve not to abandon our children, thereby providing them with as much security as we are able. Collective solutions do work and have enabled us to survive. We demand and deserve more support.

Recommended Reading

Understanding substance use

Galvani, S. (2012) *Supporting People with Alcohol and Drug Problems: Making a Difference*. Bristol, UK: Policy Press.

Phillips, R. (ed.) (2004) *Children Exposed to Parental Substance Misuse*. London: BAAF (see especially chapters by Plant, Cairns and Archer).

Grandparental kinship care

Grandparents Plus (2016) *Kinship Care: State of the Nation 2016*. Accessed on 21/09/18 at www.grandparentsplus.org.uk/kinship-care-state-of-the-nation-2016.

Reparenting

Archer, C. and Gordon, C. (2006) *New Families, Old Scripts: A Guide to the Language of Trauma and Attachment in Adoptive Families*. London: Jessica Kingsley Publishers.

Gordon, C. and Grant, E. (n.d.) *Developmental Parenting: Parenting Traumatised Children*. Accessed on 21/09/18 at www.parentingacross scotland.org/publications/essays-about-parenting.

Hughes, D. (2012) *Parenting a Child with Emotional and Behavioural Difficulties*. London: British Agencies for Adoption and Fostering.

Lyons, S. (2017) *The Repair of Early Trauma: A 'Bottom Up' Approach*. Accessed on 20/02/18 at http://beaconhouse.org.uk/developmental trauma/the-repair-of-early-trauma.

Schools/education

Bomber, L.M. (2007) *Inside I'm Hurting: Practical Strategies for Supporting Children with Attachment Difficulties in Schools.* London: Worth Publishing.

Trauma

Levy, T. and Orlans, M. (2014) *Attachment, Trauma and Healing* (second edition). London: Jessica Kingsley Publishers.

Siegel, D. (1999) *The Developing Mind.* New York: Guilford Press.

Voss, A. (2011) *Understanding Your Child's Sensory Signals* (third edition). ISBN 1466263536. CreateSpace Independent Publishing Platform (Amazon).

Sources of Help for Grandparents Raising Children

Most people look to websites for information these days, and this is advised if you find yourself in the position of taking on your grandchildren without any support. First of all you need to share what is happening with friends and family, even if the circumstances are painful. Where you find your grandchildren at serious risk, you need to contact police and/or Social Services to protect yourself and the children.

Legal status and financial support

It is advisable to clarify your legal position. Look up official and other sites for information on:

Kinship care (Family and Friends foster parenting):

www.gov.uk/looking-after-someone-elses-child

Child Arrangement Orders (which used to be called Residence Orders): www.yorkchildcare.proceduresonline.com explains the terms and the assessment for allowances.

Special Guardianship Orders:

www.gov.uk/government/Special_Guardianship_statutory_guidance.pdf

Amendments in 2016 allowed Special Guardians to apply to the Adoption Support Fund to cover the cost of therapeutic support for children:

www.adoptionsupportfund.co.uk/Parents

Financial support may be attached to these positions, although it is often discretionary or means-tested. Your local Social Services may have to be involved to support you in any application. The general sites below offer advice on benefits and tax credits.

Health and education

If you have concerns about your grandchildrens' health, including their mental health, you need to approach a GP, who may refer you to a paediatrician or to Child and Adolescent Mental Health Services (CAMHS). You should seek support from the children's school, school nurses or health visitors. Informing the school of the children's situation will allow you to get more understanding from teachers and, if necessary, help from their special educational needs coordinator (all schools have them).

Drug treatment

You may have concerns about your grandchildren's parents and the impact of substance use on families. In every local area there are drug services that may offer support to carers and families as well as to users, and also provide advice and information on drug use and treatment. For information, check out:

www.nhs.uk/livewell/drugs/pages/drugtreatment.aspx

www.nhs.Service-Search/Drug treatment520services/LocationsSearch/340

Therapeutic help

Apart from CAMHS there are many organisations and individuals offering therapeutic help for traumatised children and families. Most of these charge fees, though it is sometimes possible to get funding through educational or health bodies or, for those with SGOs, the Adoption Support Fund. There are a huge variety of therapies on offer and it is wise to do some research before committing to treatment. A review of several kinds of treatment can be found in Archer, C., Drury, C. and Hills, J. (2015) *Healing the Hidden Hurts: Transforming Attachment and Trauma Theory into Effective Practice with Families, Children and Adults.* London: Jessica Kingsley Publishers.

Support and general information

If you are looking for general support, information and advice, the following sites are extremely helpful:

Grandparents Plus: www.grandparentsplus.org.uk

> A national charity supporting thousands of grandparents and kinship carers with legal and financial advice and information; it also shares personal accounts of problems faced and overcome. A list of local support groups is available.

Family Rights Group: www.frg.org.uk

> A long-standing national non-profit organisation offering help and advice about the rights of families and children who are in need, at risk or in care.

Index